BELVEDERE SCHOOL GDST

646.14

The Belvedere Academy

This book is due for return on or before that last date shown below.

D0490225

THE
SAMPLER
MOTIF
BOOK

THE SAMPLER MOTIF BOOK

Brenda Keyes

In needle works there doth great knowledge rest.
A fine conceit thereby full soone is showne:
A drowsie braine this skill cannot digest,
Paine spent on such, in vaine awaie is throne:
They must be careful, diligent and wise,
In needle workes that beare away the prise.

From *A Booke of Curious and Strange
Inventions called the first part of Needleworkes*
published by William Barley in 1596.

David & Charles

For Irene and Jim Keyes,
with grateful thanks and much love

A DAVID & CHARLES BOOK
Text, designs and charts Copyright © Brenda Keyes 1995
Photography Copyright © David & Charles 1995
First published 1995

Brenda Keyes has asserted her right to be identified as author of this work
in accordance with the Copyright, Designs and Patents Act 1988.
All rights reserved. No part of this publication may be reproduced, stored in a
retrieval system, or transmitted, in any form or by any means, electronic or
mechanical, by photocopying, recording or otherwise, without prior permission
in writing from the publisher.

A catalogue record for this book is available from the British Library.

ISBN 0 7153 0252 3

Designed by Malcolm Couch
Printed in Italy by New Interlitho SpA
for David & Charles
Brunel House Newton Abbot Devon

Contents

Introduction

The main aim of this book is to show the enormous potential of the sampler as a source of inspiration for needlework design. I have always had an all-consuming passion for samplers, stemming, I feel, from not only their obvious charm, but also the wealth of design possibilities contained within those meticulously executed borders. Consider the composition of an 'average' sampler (I use the word tentatively, as designs are so diverse), comprising border, alphabets, verse and spot motifs. Borders range from a simple backstitch line to intricate and complex creations that, in some instances, can stand on their own, maybe needing only a simple verse to complete the design. Alphabets, too, seem to revel in extremes, from the totally uniform understated variety – much in evidence on Quaker samplers – to the wonderfully exuberant floral extravagances beloved by French needlewomen of the last century. Verses range from dour warnings of impending death, to sweet sentiment and romanticism, religion, obedience and, occasionally, even humour! This example – 'In reading this if any faults you see, Mend them yourself and find no fault in me' – is proof, if any were needed, that not all samplers were a labour of love.

Motifs used throughout the ages include an enormous variety of subjects. *The Needle's Excellency* a 17th-century pattern book by John Taylor ('wherein are divers admirable workes wrought with the needle. Newly invented and cut in copper for the pleasure and profit of the industrious'), contains the following verse:

'Flowers, Plants and Fishes
Beasts, Birds, Flyes and Bees,
Hills, Dales, Plains, Pastures,
Skies, Seas, Rivers, Trees.
There's nothing ne'er at hand or farthest sought
But with the needle may be shap'd and wrought.'

This verse embodies my feelings on the subject admirably!

Some months ago, while happily browsing in a large dilapidated junk shop (to describe it as an antique shop would, I fear, contravene the Trades Descriptions Act!), I spotted an extremely moth-eaten, damp-spotted but 'promising' sampler right at the very back of the shop. Climbing over several awkwardly-placed and lethal-looking antiquities to get to it, I aroused the attention of the shopkeeper who, anxious to avoid catastrophe, nimbly leapt over the said antiquities and retrieved it for me.

'Is it the frame you're after, then?' he enquired knowledgeably!

'No,' I replied, thoroughly taken aback at the notion that my moth-eaten treasure wasn't recognised for the prize it *clearly* was.

'It's actually the rather beautiful sampler that's taking up space in it!'

Thoroughly chastened (I like to think) and hoping for a sale (a more likely explanation!), he proceeded to admire and compliment my dust-shrouded 'find'. I left the shop with my sampler carefully wrapped in the finest newspaper, leaving the shopkeeper looking extremely puzzled. Perhaps it had something to do with my retreating remark, that not only was my purchase an unusual piece, but much more important than that, it had great potential! Perhaps if he should stumble across this book someday (hopefully not in his shop!), he will understand.

You will notice that at the end of most of the projects in this book, there is an 'alternatives' section. This offering is borne out of sheer frustration – I can always think of many more adaptations and uses for the projects than there would ever be time to stitch and therefore show in the book. These alternatives are merely suggestions for either adapting the design, or taking it one stage further. Hopefully, they will fire your imagination and inspire you to create some wonderful designs of your own. Further inspiration can be found in almost any sampler, old or new. I hope this book may encourage you to take a fresh look at the subject and explore the possibility of using elements of sampler design to create 'divers admirable workes' of your own.

Brenda Keyes 1995

Workbox

Most of the projects in this book use the technique of counted cross stitch, where the design is worked from a chart rather than being printed on fabric or canvas. The technique involved in 'reading' the chart and then 'translating' it to the fabric is an easy one to master and, once understood, will open up a host of exciting possibilities. Not only will you be able to work from any counted cross stitch chart, but you will also find it easy to adapt, enlarge, reduce and eventually create designs of your own easily and quickly.

Understanding Charts

There are many different types of charts – black and white, hand-drawn, computer-generated, coloured squares or symbols, or coloured squares with symbols. However, if this list sounds complicated and daunting, fear not! The method for

'translating' all of them is the same. One square on the chart, containing a symbol or colour, represents one stitch (usually a cross stitch) on your fabric. Figure 1 and the picture below show clearly how the chart has been 'translated' on to the fabric.

The blank squares on your chart mean that this area is unworked (one very good reason I am sure for the huge popularity of cross stitch – no unending acres of beige ever-looming in the background to fill in!). The straight black lines surrounding a motif indicate back stitch. They will add impact to your design and will often help to define areas that would otherwise blend into each other. Black is usually suggested for outlining but is sometimes too harsh, in which case a softer shade of grey or brown, or any darker shade of a colour already used, is more appropriate. Unless the design is worked in one colour only, a key will be given to indicate which colours to use for each stitch.

Figure 1: Chart for Bird in a bush motif.

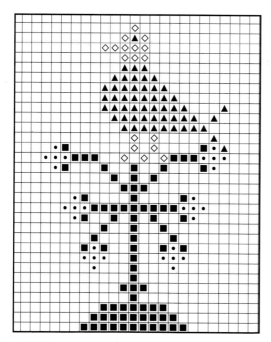

Key   DMC

◇◇ / ◇◇	370	Olive green	■■ / ■■ 500 Dark green
▲▲ / ▲▲	300	Chocolate brown	∴∴ / ∴∴ 760 Pink

Bird in a bush: The finished embroidery.

Threads

The vast range of threads available to the stitcher today, offered in an enormous choice of colours, means almost unlimited design possibilities. The most commonly used thread for counted cross stitch is stranded cotton (floss). It is treated by a process known as mercerisation, which gives it a polished sheen like silk. The advantage of stranded cotton is that the strands can be separated and recombined in any number to achieve different effects. As the cotton (floss) has six strands, many variations are possible. Two strands are commonly used for cross stitch, although one strand can be used over one thread of fabric to create delicate effects or to give emphasis when outlining in back stitch. One strand over one thread is also used for working long verses on samplers. This effectively reduces the size of the verse by half and eliminates the possibility of swamping the overall design.

There is no reason to limit yourself to the sole use of stranded cotton (floss). Wonderful effects can be achieved by substituting different threads. Try experimenting with threads you may not have used before – perlé cotton, flower threads, metallic thread, fine wool (yarn), viscose rayon thread – the list is endless. A somewhat ordinary piece of work can be totally transformed by the substitution or addition of some of the more unusual threads.

Perlé cotton is a highly mercerised, twisted, non-divisible, lustrous cotton thread available in a skein or a ball. Crewel wool (yarn) is a fine, smooth, 2-ply wool (yarn). Flower thread is a non-divisible, matt-finish thread made of 100 per cent cotton. Marlitt is a 4-ply, viscose rayon thread with a high sheen. The projects in this book use DMC stranded cotton (floss) unless otherwise specified. There is a DMC to Anchor conversion chart on page 124 for those who wish to use Anchor threads. All perlé cottons used are No 5.

Using Space-dyed or Variegated Thread

Wonderful effects can be achieved if these threads are used sympathetically. A simple design (a sampler motif for example) can be transformed by substituting this type of thread for a single colour. When using variegated thread (where the colour gradually changes from a very pale to a dark shade of the same colour), it is important to select the lengths so that the gradual change of colour is followed throughout your stitching, that is, do not place dark thread next to light. Beautifully subtle effects can be achieved if the colours merge gradually. On the other hand, some space-dyed

threads are dyed with sudden and dramatic changes of colour at quite short intervals, giving a totally different look. For both types of thread, it is important to complete each cross individually, and not work a line of half crosses and then complete by working back along the line.

Thread Storage

Storing your threads in an organised and efficient manner will enable you to see and select threads at a glance. There are many methods of thread storage, ranging from cards with holes punched in them to hold cut skeins, storage boxes with cards to wrap threads around, and sophisticated thread organisers that store threads in plastic pockets which are then housed in a binder. Whichever method you choose (including your own versions of the above), storing your threads carefully will ensure that they are clean, tangle free and freely available for selection.

Needles

You will need blunt tapestry needles for all types of counted needlework. The most commonly used sizes are 22, 24 and 26. The size selected will depend on the fabric used, for example, size 22 for 8-count Aida, size 26 for fine 30- to 36-count linen. The needle should offer a little pressure when passed through the fabric, and should not be able to drop right through the hole. Special long, fine needles are available for beading. Always try to keep an assortment of needles in stock, as it is infuriating not to be able to start your project for the lack of the appropriate needle.

Fabrics

Counted needlework requires an evenweave fabric, that is, a fabric that has the same number of threads vertically as horizontally. Such fabrics are described by the number of threads or blocks per inch (2.5cm), usually known as the count. This count will determine the finished size of the design. A wonderful variety of evenweave fabrics is now available for counted needlework, with two main types - Aida and linen. Aida fabrics are constructed in blocks, which makes counting easier and prevents uneven stitching, especially for beginners. Various types of Aida and linen fabrics have been used for the projects in this book. Aida fabrics include: Ainring, which is woven to form blocks of four threads, with 18 blocks to the inch (2.5cm); Rustico, available in 14- or 18-count, which is a naturally woven cotton fabric with a country feel; Hardanger, which is a cotton fabric woven with pairs of threads, usually 22 pairs to the inch (2.5cm).

Linen fabrics include: Edinburgh linen, a 36-count, high quality linen; Belfast linen, of similar quality but in 32-count; Dublin linen, a 25-count linen woven from fine quality flax; and Cork linen, a 19-count linen, made from strong bleached flax.

Aida, linen and even perforated paper (much loved by the Victorians) are available in a wide range of colours. Do try experimenting — you need not restrict yourself to white, beige or cream. Working your design on a coloured background will bring a different dimension to your work instantly. You could even try dyeing your own fabrics with one of the proprietary makes of dye, or really go back to basics and research methods of dyeing fabrics with natural dyes such as madder (or the more readily available onion skins!).

Fabric Allowance

It is essential to allow enough fabric surrounding the design area for stretching and framing. As a general rule, 4-6in (10-15cm) will be sufficient, although smaller pieces such as brooches, miniatures and cards will not require this much excess. The information following shows how to calculate the amount of fabric required for a design (or alternative fabrics with different thread counts). Once you have mastered the technique of calculating this way, you will find it an easy task to select the correct amount of fabric required for counted work. Always measure your fabric carefully and cut along a thread line using sharp dressmaking scissors. There are a number of methods you can use to prevent the cloth from fraying: oversew the edges by hand; machine the edges using a zig-zag stitch; bind the edges with tape (not masking tape as it can pull threads when being removed and also leave a nasty sticky residue); or use a commercially made material called Fray-check, which is applied to the edges of the fabric.

Calculating Quantities of Alternative Fabrics

Cross Stitching on Linen over Two Threads

For example: 25 threads per inch (2.5cm) linen with design area 100 stitches x 50 wide. Divide the number of vertical stitches in the design area by the stitch count of the fabric and multiply by 2. This will give you the size of the design area in inches (or centimetres). Repeat this procedure for the horizontal stitches.

Thus:

$$\frac{100}{25} = 4 \times 2 = 8\text{in (20.5cm)}$$

$$\frac{50}{25} = 2 \times 2 = 4\text{in (10cm)}$$

So the design area is 8 x 4in (20.5 x 10cm).

Add 4-6in (10-15cm) for finishing, and the fabric required is 12 x 8in (30.5 x 20.5cm).

Cross Stitching on Block Fabrics such as Aida or over one Thread of Linen

For example: 10-count Aida with design area 100 stitches high x 50 wide. Divide the number of vertical stitches in the design area by the stitch count of the fabric and this will give you the design area in inches (or centimetres). Repeat this procedure for the horizontal stitches.

Thus:

$$\frac{100}{10} = 10\text{in (25.5cm)}$$

$$\frac{50}{10} = 5\text{in (12.5cm)}$$

So the design area is 10 x 5in (25.5 x 12.5cm).

Add 4-6in (10-15cm) for finishing, and the fabric required is 14 x 9in (35 x 23cm).

Hoops and Frames

If you decide to use an embroidery hoop — and they can be a very helpful aid to accurate stitching — always use one that is big enough to house the complete design comfortably. This will ensure that the hoop never needs to be placed over any stitching and will thus avoid spoiling the completed work with pulled and snagged stitches. To prevent your fabric slipping about, it is advisable to bind the inner hoop with white bias binding secured with a few stitches.

Another way to protect your work from hoop marks is to place a piece of tissue paper between the fabric and hoop then tear away the middle section to expose the area to be worked. Hoops tend to leave crease marks that are almost impossible to remove, so always remember to remove the hoop every time you finish working.

Larger pieces of work will require a rectangular frame. They come in many sizes including large free-standing floor frames. Some have the added benefit of a magnifying light. After the side edges of the fabric have been bound with tape or hemmed to strengthen them, the top and bottom edges of the fabric are sewn to the webbing which is attached to the rollers of the frame. It is important to ensure that the fabric is placed evenly in the frame, as if it is sewn in unevenly it will become distorted. The frame is then assembled and the side edges laced to the stretchers with very long thread (see Figure 2).

A quicker and easier, though just as effective, way of keeping your fabric taut, is to use ready-made rectangular frames which are available in a variety of sizes from some embroidery shops. The fabric is stapled straight on to the frame (or attached with drawing pins), thus saving a great deal of time and effort. Although less elegant than

roller frames, I feel they have many advantages — there are no protruding corners to catch your thread on, they are lighter to hold, easier to store and more portable. For really large pieces of work, however, where the overall size would rule out the possibility of holding the entire framed piece comfortably, a roller frame would be more appropriate.

Adhesives

For some of the projects you will need to use glue, for example, when sticking a piece of embroidery in a fold-over card. There are many adhesives available, but I always prefer to use UHU glue, which is recommended for use with fabric and dries on impact. Also the fumes associated with this type of product are less obvious and troublesome in UHU.

Enlarging and Reducing Charted Designs

Charted designs are extremely versatile and very easy to enlarge or reduce in size. There are a number of ways to do this.

1 Consider every square in the design to be two, three or even four stitches square instead of one. For example, to triple the design size, work a block of stitches three by three for every one stitch shown.

2 Work the stitches over two, three or even four threads or blocks of fabric (Aida commonly). For example, if you work over four threads instead of two, the design will double in size. Likewise, if the instructions state that the design is worked in cross stitch over two threads of linen and you work over just one thread in either cross stitch or tent stitch, the design size will be halved.

3 The fabric chosen will also play a large part in determining the size of the design. For example, working over one block of 11-count Aida as opposed to working the same design over one thread of linen 36 threads per inch (2.5cm), will increase the design size dramatically.

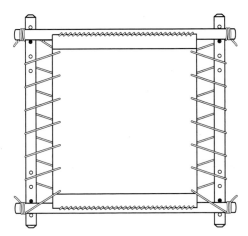

Fig 2: A rectangular frame.

By using any of the methods described here, it will enable you to make much more use of the motifs, alphabets and borders shown in this book. For example, the repeated strawberry motif used for the pincushion on page 99, is worked over just one thread of fine canvas in a fine crewel wool (yarn). Worked in tapestry wool (yarn) on a larger gauge canvas over two threads, in cross stitch it would easily translate into a cushion. Likewise, any of the larger motifs worked over two threads could be worked over one on a fine linen and used for brooches, bookmarks or miniatures, etc.

How to Begin Working

Finding the Centre of the Fabric

Fold your fabric in half and half again and crease lightly. Tack (baste) along these lines in a contrasting sewing thread. The centre of the fabric is where the lines cross. Most instructions suggest that you begin work at this point – this is to ensure that your work is distributed evenly, avoiding the horrible possibility of working off the edge of the fabric! However, if you want to start work at, say, the top left-hand corner of the design (and this does seem to be a more logical alternative with designs that include a border), you must carefully calculate where to start by deducting the design size from your fabric size and positioning accordingly. For example, if your fabric size is 12 x 10in (30.5 x 25.5cm) and your design size 8 x 6in (20.5 x 15cm), you will have 4in (10cm) of spare fabric. You should therefore measure 2in (5cm) down from the top edge and 2in (5cm) from the side edge and begin work here.

Starting to Stitch

The following list of do's and don'ts will ensure that you achieve a perfect start and a perfect finish.

1 Cut your thread no longer than 12-18in (30.5-45.5cm).

2 When using stranded cotton (floss) always separate and untwist all six strands before selecting the number of strands required. (The amount will depend on the fabric used.) This method will ensure that the threads lie flatter and give greater coverage.

3 Never use a knot to begin stitching. Knots can pull through the fabric and will give a bumpy finish which will spoil the appearance of your work. To begin stitching previously unworked fabric, bring the needle up through the fabric leaving about an inch (2.5cm) of thread at the back. Holding this thread in place, work three or four stitches until the trailing thread is caught and secured. To begin a new thread on fabric which has been previously stitched, simply run the needle through the loops of three or four stitches at the back of the work near to where you wish to begin stitching. Bring the needle up at the required place and begin.

4 Be careful not to pull stitches too tightly. They should sit evenly on the fabric – tension is just as important in embroidery as in knitting.

5 Make sure that all top stitches in cross stitch are in the same direction to ensure a smooth even finish.

6 Remember to 'drop' your needle every four to five stitches. This will take the twist out of the thread and avoid tangles.

7 The method for finishing/securing a thread is much the same as starting. Leaving yourself enough thread to finish, take the needle through to the back of the work. Run the needle through the back loop of three or four stitches and snip off the thread close to the stitching.

Working the Project

Stitch instructions are given in the Stitch Directory on page 123. Further skills, such as finishing, mounting and framing a completed piece of embroidery, making a fold-over card, or a twisted cord and tassels, are described at the back of the book (see Finishing Techniques, pages 118-122). For suppliers of the materials used, refer to page 127.

Band Sampler

The 17th century has been described as the 'Golden Age of the Sampler'. Many early samplers were real works of art, often over a yard (1 metre) long. They were rolled on to a small ivory rod, made for the purpose, for storage. This example is worked in cross stitch and back stitch on linen, and although not as long and narrow as early examples, this sampler features many of the border patterns and alphabets that would have appeared on them.

Design size: 9¼ x 12¼ in (23.5 x 31cm)
Stitch count: 115 x 154

13 x 16in (33 x 40.5cm) natural Dublin linen, 25 threads per inch (2.5cm)
Stranded cottons (floss) as shown in the key

Use 2 strands of stranded cotton (floss) over 2 threads of linen, except for the verse, remaining words and date which are worked over 1 thread of linen.

1 Find the centre of the design and work outwards from this point following the chart.

2 Using the main chart on pages 16 and 17, first work the main body of the design in cross stitch and back stitch over two threads of linen. To add the verse, words and date, use the main chart to position the first letter on each line and then follow the additional chart (below), working over just one thread of linen.

3 Substitute your own name and date using the alphabets in the sampler. Work out your details on graph paper and position as shown.

4 Stretch, mount and frame as required (see pages 118 -122).

ALTERNATIVES
■ Add more borders and alphabets from the book to make a longer band sampler.

■ Use any of the borders to decorate household linen. The backstitch border would look stunning worked in black on white table napkins.

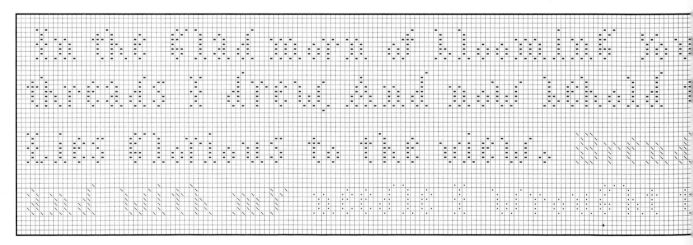

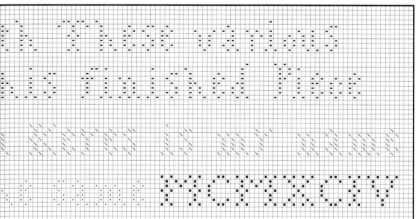

Band Sampler Lettering

Key	DMC	
	300	Chocolate brown
	890	Dark green
	434	Warm brown
	3371	Very dark brown

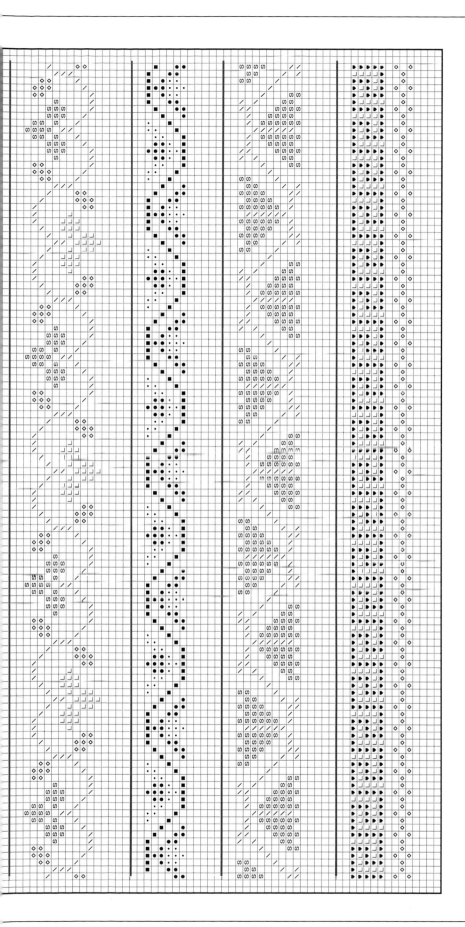

Work backstitch in 3371 Very dark brown
See additional chart on pages 14 and 15
for verse/name etc., and insert where
indicated by the red lines

Band Sampler

Key DMC

⚋	890	Dark green
◇	732	Sage green
s	347	Dull red
⌐	680	Dark gold
‖	300	Chocolate brown

▶	413	Dark grey
••	926	Light slate blue
■	3371	Very dark brown
⋮	434	Warm brown

Bush with Repeat Pattern Border

*The addition of an elaborate and subtly shaded border transforms
this simple motif of a bush into a most unusual piece.
It is worked in cross stitch on evenweave fabric.*

Design size: 5 x 5in (12.5 x 12.5cm)
Stitch count: 81 x 81

9 x 9in (23 x 23cm) natural Floba, 18 threads per
inch (2.5cm)
Stranded cottons (floss) as shown in the key

Use 2 strands of stranded cotton (floss) over 1
thread of fabric.

1 Find the centre of the design and work outwards from this point following the chart.

2 Stretch, mount and frame as required (see
pages 118-122).

ALTERNATIVES

■ Substitute bright primary colours for those used
in the border, and use the design as a basis for a
birth sampler. Add the child's name, date of birth,
etc, using the additional alphabets on pages 114-
115 and working out your details in pencil on
graph paper.

■ Substitute any other sampler motif of a suitable
size from the book for the centre panel.

■ Work the border design in cross stitch with
wool (yarn) on canvas to make a belt. Repeat the
pattern for the required length.

Detail of repeat pattern border.

Bush with Repeat Pattern Border

Key	DMC						
	355	Dark rust		597	Soft turquoise	957	Bright pink
	924	Antique blue		434	Warm brown	422	Light gold
	3041	Mauve		3371	Very dark brown	926	Light slate blue
				315	Plum	730	Sage green

Page Keepers

This simple but effective idea uses small pieces of perforated paper and ribbon or bias binding. Worked in cross stitch, a page keeper would be the perfect addition to give with a book to make the gift really special. Choose any of the designs shown here, or indeed any motif from the book. Tailor the design either to the book itself, for example the bunch of grapes for a book on wine, the ABC for a child's book, etc, or work the recipient's initials using one of the alphabets from the book.

Page Keepers

Small pieces of perforated paper (the exact size depends on your chosen design)

Stranded cottons (floss) as shown in the key
Ribbon or bias binding
Glue/impact adhesive

Use 2 strands of cotton (floss) over 1 block of perforated paper.

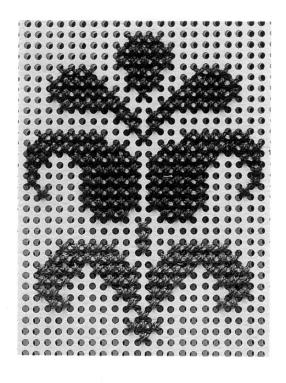

1 Choose your design, then count the number of squares vertically and horizontally to assess the size of perforated paper needed. Cut two pieces the same size, allowing for trimming and gluing the corner edges together.

2 Find the centre of the design and match it to the centre of the perforated paper. Work outwards from this point following the chart.

3 Cut two pieces of contrasting ribbon or bias binding the same length as the right-hand corner edges and apply a little glue to the wrong side of each piece. Place the unworked piece of perforated paper on to the back of the worked piece, matching the holes. Fold each piece of glued ribbon in turn on to one of the corner edges and press into place.

4 Trim any rough edges, or cut to shape if you wish (see designs).

ALTERNATIVES

■ To make an 'heirloom' page keeper, work a complex design (an ecclesiastical design for a family bible for example) over one thread of fine linen. Make up as described, but fold the outer edges under and line with parchment paper.

■ Use any of the motifs shown here to decorate a small trinket pot lid.

■ Work one of the motifs on a longer piece of perforated paper to make a bookmark.

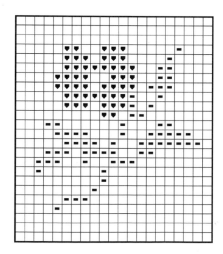

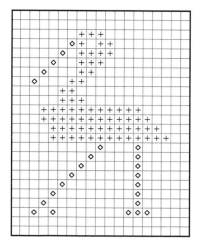

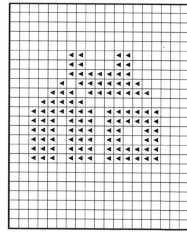

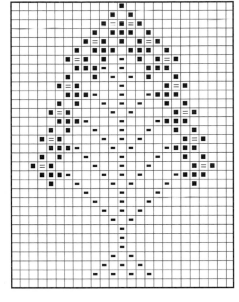

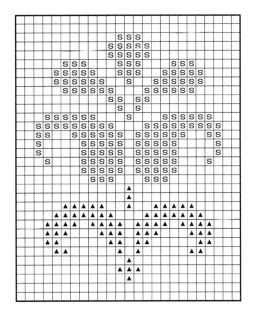

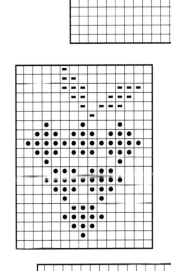

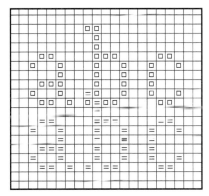

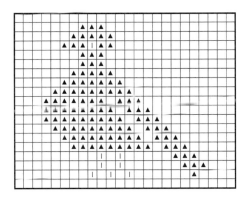

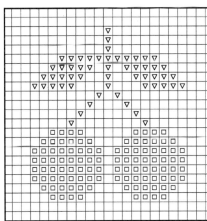

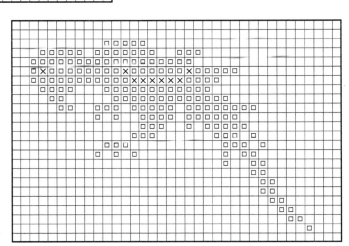

Page Keepers

Key	DMC				
▢▢ / ▢▢	321	Red	•• / •• 327	Dark purple	++ / ++ Ecru
═══ / ═══	444	Bright yellow	×× / ×× D282	Gold thread	‖‖ / ‖‖ 3371 Very dark brown
■■ / ■■	552	Purple	SS / SS 315	Plum	▼▼ / ▼▼ 356 Apricot
═■ / ═■	730	Sage green	▲▲ / ▲▲ 3768	Blue	◀◀ / ◀◀ 823 Navy
			◇◇ / ◇◇ 3378	Pale apricot	▽▽ / ▽▽ 890 Dark green

Cherub Card and Picture

Cherub motifs can be found in many of the sampler designs of the past. They were particularly beloved by the Victorians who seemed to revel in romance and sentimentality. 'Nothing wrong with that!' I say and, judging by the huge popularity of all things Victorian over the last decade, I feel I am not alone. The picture and card are worked in cross stitch on linen.

The Picture
Design size: 4³/₄ x 2in (12 x 5cm)
Stitch count: 71 x 30

7 x 5in (18 x 12.5cm) cream Belfast linen,
32 threads per inch (2.5cm)
Stranded cottons (floss) as shown in the key
Frame

Use 2 strands of stranded cotton (floss) over 2
threads of linen for the cherub motif, and 1 strand
over 1 thread of linen for the initial.

THE PICTURE

1 Find the centre of the design and work outwards from this point following the chart.

2 Choose your initial from the alphabet shown
on page 96, and centre within the heart, by
counting the number of squares horizontally and
vertically on the chart and matching the mid-
point of the initial to the mid-point of the heart.
(NB: The initial is worked over only one thread of
linen.)

3 Stretch, mount and frame as required (see
pages 118-122).

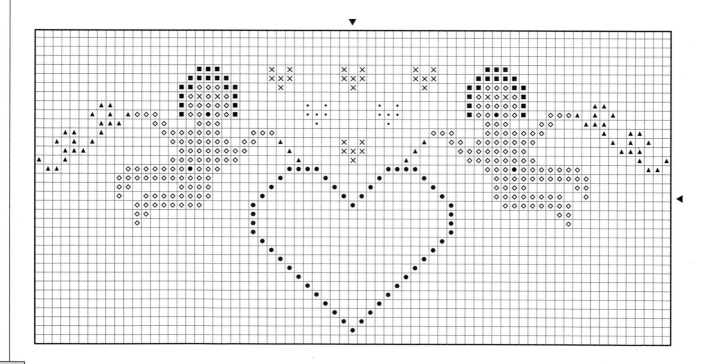

The Card
Design size: 3 1/8 x 2in (8 x 5cm)
Stitch count: 47 x 30

5 x 4in (12.5 x 10cm) cream Belfast linen, 32 threads
per inch (2.5cm)
Stranded cottons (floss) as shown in the key
Purchased card

Use 2 strands of stranded cotton (floss) over 2
threads of linen for the cherub motif, and 1 strand
over 1 thread of linen for the initial.

Cherub Card and Picture
Key   DMC

◦◦ / ◦◦	842	Flesh	×× / ××	927	Pale slate blue
■■ / ■■	434	Warm brown	▲▲ / ▲▲	926	Light slate blue
∴∴ / ∴∴	223	Deep pink	⋮⋮ / ⋮⋮	818	Very light pink

THE CARD

1 Follow steps 1 and 2 as described opposite.

2 Insert into the card following the instructions
given in Finishing Techniques (page 118).

ALTERNATIVES

■ Work the design in cross stitch with wool (yarn)
on a large mesh canvas to make a wonderfully
romantic Victorian cushion. Edge with cream lace
and add ribbon bows.

■ Use the design to decorate the lid of a trinket
pot.

■ Enlarge the heart and transform the design into
a baby announcement by adding the baby's name,
date of birth, weight, etc, using a small backstitch
alphabet (see page 114).

Birds and Carnations

The intricate balance of this design, with its over-large birds and remarkably small ones nestling in the foliage, make for perfect symmetry.
No regard whatsoever is given to scale, giving this design a charming naiveté typical of samplers in general. The picture is worked in tent stitch on linen and the cushion is worked in cross stitch on evenweave fabric.

The Picture
Design size: 6³/₄ x 5³/₄in (17 x 14.5cm)
Stitch count: 131 x 100

10¹/₂ x 9¹/₂in (26.5 x 24cm) cream Cork linen,
19 threads per inch (2.5cm)
Stranded cottons (floss) as shown in the key

Use 3 strands of cotton (floss) over 1 thread of linen.

THE PICTURE

1 Find the centre of the design and work outwards from this point following the chart. As tent stitch tends to distort fabric, the use of a frame is advisable.

2 Stretch, mount and frame as required (see pages 118-122).

Using Tent Stitch
This method of stitching tent stitch over one thread of linen has much to recommend it and can be applied to other charted designs. The advantages of working in this way are that the design is completed in half the time, and, unlike working on canvas, the background does not have to be covered.

The size of the finished design will obviously have to be taken into consideration; usually this method is employed to reduce the size of a design. If you use a larger mesh linen, however, such as Cork with 19 threads per inch (2.5cm), this will not only produce a finished size which is comparable to 18-count Aida, but will also lessen the possibility of eyestrain which can occur when working on fine linen.

The Cushion
Design size: 15¹/₂ x 12in (39.5 x 30.5cm)
Stitch count: 131 x 100

17 x 17in (43 x 43cm) natural Floba fabric,
18 threads per inch (2.5cm)
Stranded cottons (floss) as shown in the key
17 x 17in (43 x 43cm) cotton backing fabric
Matching sewing thread
10in (25.5cm) zip (optional)
Cushion pad, 16in (40.5cm) square
A 60in (152.5cm) length of plaited wool or twisted cord in matching shades

Use 4 strands of cotton (floss) over 2 threads of fabric.

THE CUSHION

1 Find the centre of the design, match to the centre of the fabric and work outwards from this point following the chart.

2 Pin and tack (baste) the embroidery and backing fabric right sides together. Machine or hand stitch, leaving a large enough gap on the bottom edge to take the cushion pad. Oversew or zig-zag the seams to strengthen them.

3 If you have chosen to insert a zip, add at this stage. Alternatively, simply turn the cushion right side out, insert the cushion pad and close the gap with small invisible stitches.

4 Sew the plait or twisted cord to the edge of the cushion, where the embroidery and backing fabric meet by hand, using a matching thread.

ALTERNATIVES

■ Work the design in wool (yarn) on canvas and make into a cushion or fire screen.

■ Use the design to decorate the lid of a needle-work box.

Nursery Triplets

These three charming pastel miniatures, based on the Nursery Picture on page 30, worked in cross stitch and back stitch on Aida fabric, will add the perfect touch to a nursery.

Design size: $1^7/_8$ x $2^1/_2$in (4.5 x 6.5cm)
Size of picture with mount: $4^1/_2$ x $4^1/_2$in (11.5 x 11.5cm)
Stitch count: 26 x 34

To make the set of three
4 x 4in (10 x 10cm) 14-count Aida fabric in pale yellow, pale pink and pale blue
Stranded cottons (floss) as shown in the key
3 pieces of cardboard $4^1/_2$ x $4^1/_2$in (11.5 x 11.5cm)
$5^1/_2$ x $16^1/_2$in (14 x 42cm) cream cotton fabric, cut into 3 pieces $5^1/_2$ x $5^1/_2$in (14 x 14 cm)

3 pieces of cardboard 3 x $3^1/_2$in (7.5 x 9cm)
Glue/impact adhesive
12 deep pink shirt buttons
18in (45.5cm) each of rose pink and pale blue narrow ribbons
3 ready-made deep mauve ribbon roses
3 plain wooden frames to fit a $4^1/_2$ x $4^1/_2$in (11.5 x 11.5cm) mount

Use 2 strands of stranded cotton (floss) over 1 block of fabric.

1 For each picture, find the centre of the design and work outwards from this point following the chart.

2 Cut an aperture measuring $2^1/_4$ x $2^3/_4$in (5.5 x 7cm) centrally in each of the larger pieces of cardboard and cover with cream cotton fabric (see Finishing Techniques, page 119).

3 After lacing each piece of embroidery on to a small piece of cardboard, position the covered mounts carefully on top of the finished pieces and glue together, or attach with masking tape.

4 Glue a shirt button face down, so that the flat side is uppermost, at each corner of the cream-covered mount. Position as shown in the photograph.

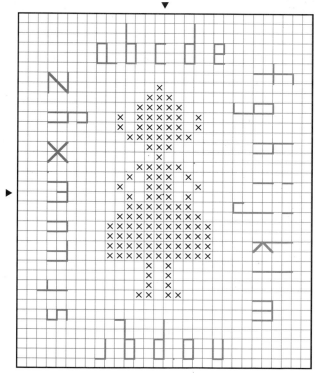

Pink colourway

Key	DMC	
×× ××	316	Mauve pink
letters	597	Soft turquoise

Blue colourway

	DMC	
×× ××	316	Mauve pink
letters	745	Soft yellow

Yellow colourway

	DMC	
×× ××	316	Mauve pink
letters	954	Pale green

The pink colourway. All three can be seen on page 33.

ALTERNATIVES

5 Make tiny ribbon bows from the pink and blue ribbons (one of each colour) and sew together. Sew a ribbon rose to the centre of the bows to cover the stitching and, after assembling the embroidery in the frame, glue into place as shown in the photograph. (See the Nursery Picture on page 30 for painting a frame.)

■ Replace the alphabet with a child's name repeated around the edge.

■ Work the design on the pocket of a blouse using waste canvas (see page 122).

■ Work the design in bright primary colours and paint a frame to match.

Home Sweet Home

The Home Sweet Home sampler has retained its popularity since Victorian times. Worked in cross stitch on linen using only five colours of cotton (floss), this particular version will look equally at home in an old or new house.

Design size: 10¹/₂ x 10³/₄in (26.5 x 27.5cm)
Stitch count: 135 x 135

14¹/₂ x 14¹/₂in (37 x 37cm) cream Dublin linen,
25 threads per inch (2.5cm)
Stranded cottons (floss) as shown in the key

Use 2 strands of cotton (floss) over 2 threads of linen.

1 Find the centre of the design and work outwards from this point following the chart.

2 Stretch, mount and frame as required (see pages 118-122).

ALTERNATIVES

■ Make the design up as a cushion with calico backing and pipe in blue.

■ Substitute the words 'Home Sweet Home' with the name of your house, or house number and name of your road, or a favourite verse or saying.

Sampler Motif Guitar Strap

Of all the many needlework gifts I have made for family and friends over the years, those that seem to have brought the most pleasure are the guitar/mandolin straps I have made for musician friends. Worked in cross stitch on a natural linen band in subtle sampler shades, this highly unusual, yet simple-to-make guitar strap will bring delight to any budding John Williams!

Design size: 3 x 39in (7.5 x 99cm) (Adjust length to suit player – choose one or more of the motifs from the chart to add length to the design)

2 lengths of natural linen band, 3in (7.5cm) wide x required length, plus 2in (5cm) for finishing
Stranded cottons (floss) as shown in the key
Matching sewing cotton
2 leather guitar strap ends removed from purchased strap (these are inexpensive and readily available from most music shops)

Use 2 strands of stranded cotton (floss) over 2 threads of natural linen band.

1 Measure 2¹/₂in (6.5cm) from the top of the linen band and begin working the two facing birds here.

2 To substitute the maker's initials for those shown, use an alphabet chart from pages 114-115, and chart your chosen initials in pencil on graph paper. Position as shown in the chart.

3 When you have worked sufficient motifs to complete the desired length, pin, tack (baste) and then oversew the side edges of the

unworked length of linen band to the wrong side of the worked length in a matching sewing thread, using small stitches. Leave the short ends open.

4 Insert the guitar strap ends, then fold the linen band in at the sides to fit. Make ¹/₂in (1.5cm) turnings at each bottom edge, enclosing the guitar strap ends, and oversew together. Finally, sew through all thicknesses in back stitch at each end, just above the guitar strap end, to keep them flat.

ALTERNATIVES
■ Work on linen and widen the design by repeating the motifs. Back with fabric to make a charming bell pull.

■ Use this design, or a combination of any of the smaller motifs in the book, to decorate a belt or pair of braces.

■ Use any of the motifs individually for greetings cards.

■ Shorten the length of the design and use for a spectacles case.

■ Use the motifs to decorate a height chart for a child (numerals can be found on pages 114-115).

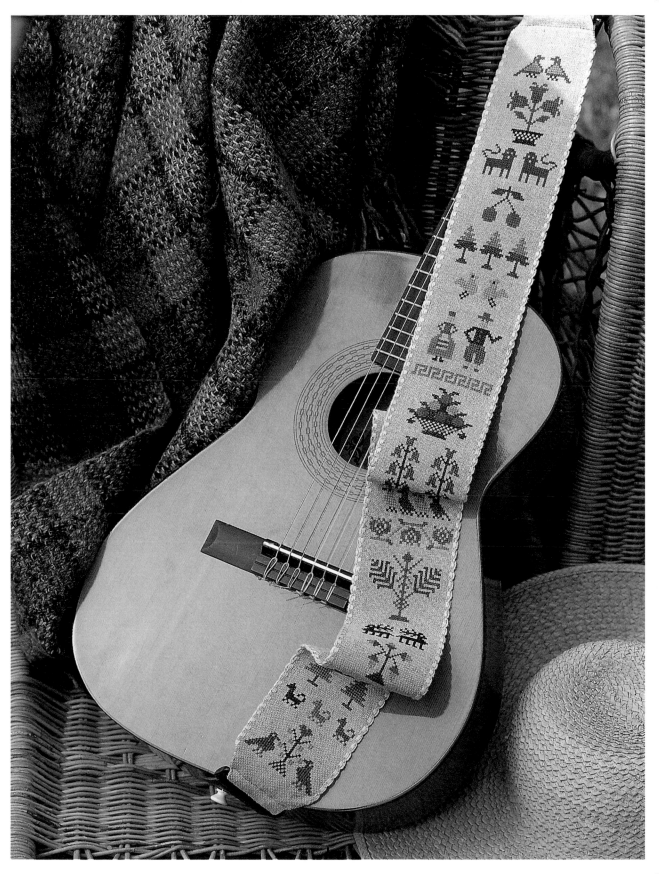

Alphabet
Sampler

Try encouraging a young member of the family to take up cross stitch by working this simple alphabet sampler. Ideal as a practice piece – girls as young as five years of age would have made similar pieces in the past – this charming little sampler would provide a perfect introduction to stitching. A beginner could substitute 14-count Rustico fabric for the linen.

Design size: 4$\frac{1}{2}$ x 6$\frac{3}{4}$in (11.5 x 17cm)
Stitch count: 62 x 95

8 x 10in (20.5 x 25.5cm) unbleached linen,
28 threads per inch (2.5cm)
Stranded cottons (floss) as shown in the key

Use 2 strands of stranded cotton (floss) over 2
threads of linen.

1   Find the centre of the design and work out-
    wards from this point following the chart.

2   Chart your name from the alphabets given
    and the date from the backstitch numerals
on page 114. Work out your details on graph
paper in pencil and position as shown.

3   Stretch, mount and frame as required (see
    pages 118 -122).

ALTERNATIVES
■ Work in pastel colours on cream linen for a
birth sampler, adding an extra line at the bottom
of the design for the date of birth.

■ Add a border to make a larger sampler.

■ Use the letters to personalise any appropriate
cross stitch design by adding your name.

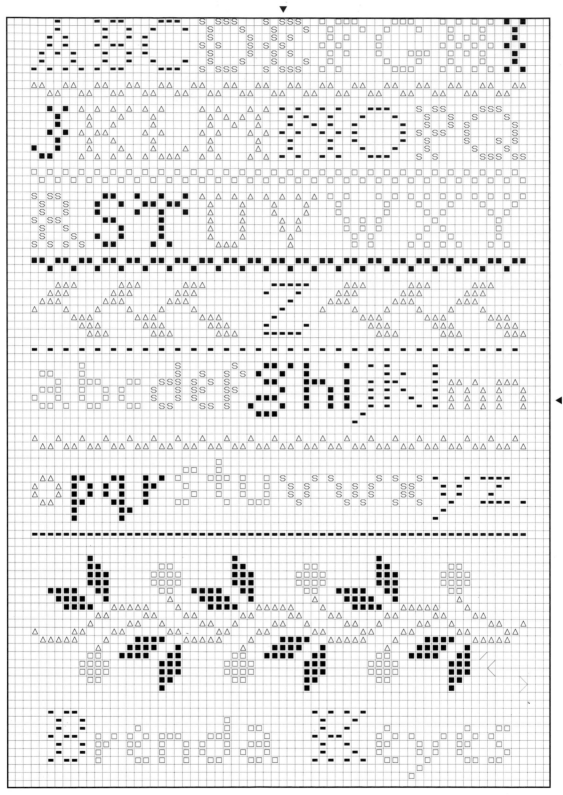

Alphabet Sampler Key DMC

⊟	823	Navy
⊡	729	Gold
⊡	355	Dark rust
⊡	732	Dark sage
⊡	890	Dark green

Carnation Cushion

This bold canvaswork cushion with its repeated carnation motif and tulip border is worked in tent stitch with subtle shades of wool (yarn) on canvas. The carnation and the tulip – both much loved designs – were frequently used throughout the last four centuries as both border and spot motifs. Symbolically, this cushion represents love, as the tulip is often associated with perfect love and the carnation with maternal love. (See pages 116–117 for further symbolic meanings of motifs.)

Design size: 13½ x 14½in (34.5 x 37cm)
Stitch count: 137 x 149

18 x 18in (45.5 x 45.5cm) white lockweave canvas, 10 holes per inch (2.5cm)
DMC Laine Colbert in colours as shown in the key
Stranded cottons (floss) as shown in the key
16 x 16in (40.5 x 40.5cm) furnishing fabric for plain backing
Matching sewing thread
10in (25.5cm) zip (optional)
Cushion pad, 14in (35.5cm) square
60in (1.5m) heavy twisted cord
2 large tassels

Use 1 strand of wool (yarn) over 1 thread of canvas.

1 Find the centre of the design and work outwards from this point following the chart. As tent stitch tends to distort canvas, it is advisable to use a frame.

2 When the main body of the design has been stitched, oversew at random, in tent stitch, some of the stitches in the carnation buds, using DMC 356 Apricot and DMC 926 Light slate blue. This will give a speckled effect and add interest to the design.

3 If the finished piece is not quite straight when completed, you will need to block (damp stretch) it (see Finishing Techniques, page 119).

4 Trim the canvas to within ³/₄in (2cm) of the embroidery, cutting across the corners diagonally to within ¹/₄in (5mm) to reduce bulk.

5 Pin and tack (baste) the embroidery and backing fabric with right sides together, trimming backing fabric to size. Machine or hand stitch together, leaving a large enough gap on the fourth side to take the cushion pad. Oversew or zig-zag the seams to strengthen them.

6 If you have chosen to insert a zip, add it at this stage. Alternatively, simply turn the cushion right side out, insert the cushion pad and close the gap with small invisible stitches.

7 Sew the twisted cord to the edge of the cushion where the embroidery meets the backing fabric, by hand, using a matching thread. Bind the edges of the cord with masking tape until you are ready to sew them to the cushion, and make sure that you stitch them down firmly, as they tend to unravel very quickly.

8 Finally, stitch one tassel securely to each corner, as shown in the photograph.

ALTERNATIVES

■ Work the design in cross stitch on linen, omitting the background colours and making up into a cushion as before.

■ Use the all-over carnation pattern to cover a footstool or chair.

■ Work the tulip border in cross stitch and use to decorate household linen – sheets, pillowcases, napkins, etc.

Carnation cushion and spectacles case.

Carnation Spectacles Case

*Worked in cross stitch on canvas,
this vibrant design would make a delightful gift. It uses the same chart as the
Carnation Cushion (see page 50), but has a somewhat different look owing to
the alternative threads that have been used. The petals of the flower are
worked in a wonderfully rich space-dyed thread, the bud and leaves in perlé
cotton and the background in wool (yarn).*

Design size: 3¹/₄ x 6¹/₂in (8 x 16.5cm)
Stitch count: 38 x 78

5 x 8in (12.5 x 20.5cm) beige 12-mesh canvas
DMC Laine Colbert 7372
Watercolours, colour 084 from the Caron collection
DMC perlé cotton (5) 744
5 x 8in (12.5 x 20.5cm) maroon velvet for backing
Matching sewing thread
8 x 8in (20.5 x 20.5cm) maroon cotton lining fabric
18in (45.5cm) narrow gold cord

Use 1 strand of wool (yarn) over 1 thread of canvas.
Do not separate the watercolour thread into
strands, but use it as it is supplied

1 Follow steps 1-4 for the Carnation Cushion
(see page 47), but leave the top edge completely open. Turn the case right side out, then
turn back the extra canvas at the top edge so that
the wrong sides are together, and tack (baste).

2 Fold the lining in half widthways and join
the side and bottom ¹/₂in (1cm) seams. Trim
and then oversew or zig-zag the seams. Insert the
lining into the case and fold under the top edges.
Stitch the lining to the case at the top edge using
small invisible stitches.

3 Sew the gold cord to the edge of the case
where the embroidery and backing meet,
using small stitches. Turn in neatly at the top edges.

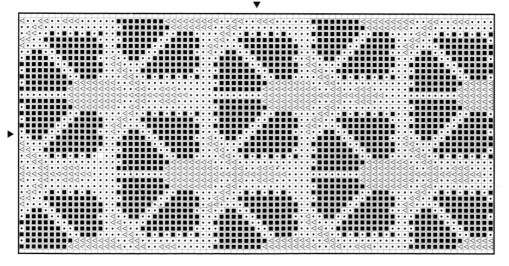

Carnation Spectacles Case
Key   DMC
744 Perlé cotton (5)

Watercolours – colour
084 from the Caron
collection

7372 Laine Colbert

Heart Tree Birth Sampler

*This delicately pretty birth sampler with hearts, flowers, tiny birds,
bows and a heart tree is sure to please. Worked in cross stitch and back stitch
on linen, it will make the perfect gift for a new baby or small child.*

Design size: 7 x 8in (18 x 20.5cm)
Stitch count: 98 x 114

11 x 12in (28 x 30.5cm) cream evenweave linen,
28 threads per inch (2.5cm)
Stranded cottons (floss) as shown in the key

Use 2 strands of stranded cotton (floss) over 2
threads of linen.

Detail of Heart Tree.

1   Measure 2in (5cm) from the top of the
fabric and 2in (5cm) in from the side and
start working the top left-hand corner of the
design at this point.

2   Work the cross stitches first, then add the
back stitches.

3   Chart your chosen name and date from the
alphabet and numerals given on pages 114-
115 in pencil on graph paper, and position as
shown on the chart.

4   Stretch, mount and frame as required (see
pages 118-122).

ALTERNATIVES

■ Work the sampler in primary colours for a boy.
This suggestion is made simply because most boys'
rooms appear to be decorated in these colours as
opposed to pastels!

■ Use a smaller backstitch alphabet (page 114)
and include more information in the centre heart,
for example, weight, place of birth, and perhaps
the parents' names.

■ Work just the centre heart shape, the child's
name and the date of birth. House in a purchased
greetings card, purpose-made for needlework,
or make your own (see page 120), for a unique
'welcome to baby' card.

■ Use the line of ducks to decorate a baby's bib,
towel, cot sheet or bathrobe, etc.

Heart Tree Birth Sampler

Key DMC

⊡⊡	818	Very pale pink
⊟⊟	926	Light slate blue
SSS	758	Pale apricot
✕✕	3348	Pale green
⋮⋮	828	Very pale blue
■■	356	Apricot

Work name/numerals in 355 Dark rust
Work the backstitch outlines in 924
Antique blue

Les Arbres

A plethora of trees adorn this unusual sampler. Worked in cross stitch on evenweave fabric, this delightfully simple design would suit a country kitchen perfectly.

Design size: 9¼ x 7in (23.5 x 18cm)
Stitch count: 163 x 124

13 x 11in (33 x 28cm) cream 18-count Davosa fabric
Stranded cottons (floss) as shown in the key

Use 2 strands of stranded cotton (floss) over 1 thread of fabric.

1 Find the centre of the design and work outwards from this point following the chart.

2 Stretch, mount and frame as required (see pages 118-122).

ALTERNATIVES

■ Choose one line of the trees as a decorative edge for place mats or napkins.

■ Work the design on canvas (in cross stitch or tent stitch) and make up as a cushion.

■ Use any of the tree motifs separately for greetings cards.

■ Select any of the tree motifs to add to a sampler.

Fruit Tree

This simple fruit tree motif, worked in cross stitch on linen,
shows that sampler motifs need not necessarily look traditional.
The addition of thread-wrapped cards as an inner mount
and cords surrounding the outer mount lift this piece
out of the ordinary.

Design size: 2¼ x 2⅞ in (5.5 x 7.5cm)
Stitch count: 31 x 39

5 x 5in (12.5 x 12.5cm) cream evenweave linen,
28 threads per inch (2.5cm)
Stranded cottons (floss) as shown in the key

For the mount:
Piece of grey card 8 x 8in (20.5 x 20.5cm)
4 pieces of card ¾ x 5½in (2 x 14cm)
1 skein DMC perlé cotton - variegated 53
Glue/impact adhesive
24in (61cm) thick gold cord
60in (1.5m) fine navy blue cord

Use 2 strands of stranded cotton (floss) over 2
threads of linen.

1 Find the centre of the design and work outwards from this point following the chart.

2 To mount the design as shown, cut a central
   aperture 5 x 5in (12.5 x 12.5cm) in the piece
of grey card.

3 Cover the narrow pieces of card with the
   variegated thread by winding tightly around,
securing the ends of the thread with impact
adhesive.

4 Apply a line of adhesive around the edge of
   the aperture at the back of the card mount

and press first the two side pieces, and then the
top and bottom pieces on to it. Leave to dry.

5 Apply a further line of adhesive approximately ¼ in (5mm) away from the edge of
the grey mount at the front of the card and leave
for one minute until the adhesive becomes tacky.
Press the gold cord on to the adhesive, starting at
the mid-point at the bottom. Trim, so that the
ends just meet and apply a little extra adhesive at
this point to prevent fraying.

6 Apply a further line of adhesive on either
   side of the gold cord, as close as possible to
it, and, using the navy cord, repeat the latter part
of step 5.

7 Cut a 6in (15cm) piece of the fine navy blue
   cord and make into a bow. Glue the bow to
the point where the ends of the cords meet.

ALTERNATIVES
■ Use this type of mount in alternate colourways
to frame any other suitable sampler motif in the
book.

■ Add a border worked in the same two colours
for a larger picture.

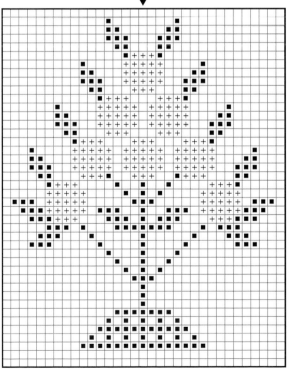

Fruit Tree
Key   DMC

   413   Dark grey

   680   Dark gold

Elizabethan Border Projects

This type of elaborate border worked in back stitch and queen stitch was very popular in Elizabethan times. Blackwork patterns were used profusely to decorate clothing – bodices, sleeves, gloves and even shoes were covered in the most intricate embroidery. Because pattern books were rare and extremely hard to obtain, intricate patterns such as this would have been worked in bands on narrow strips of linen, now known as Band Samplers, not for the decorative purpose we now associate with the working of a sampler, but in the true sense of the word – an example to work from.

The Bookmark
Design size: 2¼ x 8½in (5.5 x 21.5cm)
Stitch count: 30 x 112

11½in (29cm) unbleached linen band, 2¾in (7cm) wide, 30 threads per inch (2.5cm)
DMC stranded cotton (floss) 823 Dark navy
DMC Gold thread D282
Matching sewing cotton

Use 2 strands of stranded cotton (floss) over 2 threads of linen.

THE BOOKMARK

1 Measure 1½in (40mm) down from the top of the unbleached linen band and begin stitching the top middle 'diamond', matching the mid-point on the chart to the mid-point of the linen band (widthways).

2 Complete the design in back stitch and queen stitch following the chart.

3 When the embroidery is complete, make a ½in (1.5cm) turning at the top edge and hem stitch into place using matching cotton.

4 Fray the bottom ¾in (2cm) of the linen band.

5 Make two small tassels using stranded cotton and gold thread (see page 121). Position as shown in the photograph and attach with small invisible stitches using gold thread.

The Chequebook Cover

*The size given will fit a 9 x 3¹/₂in (23 x 9cm)
chequebook. Adjust the size as necessary to fit.*

23in (58.5cm) white linen band, 4in (10cm) wide, 30
threads per inch (2.5cm)
DMC stranded cotton (floss) 902 Dark maroon
DMC Gold thread D282
18¹/₂ x 4in (47 x 10cm) white iron-on Vilene
White sewing cotton

Use 2 strands of stranded cotton (floss) over 2
threads of linen.

THE CHEQUEBOOK COVER

1 Follow steps 1 & 2 for the bookmark, but
begin stitching 2¹/₂in (6.5cm) from the top of
the linen band.

2 When the embroidery is complete, match
the centre point of the iron-on Vilene to the
centre point of the embroidered band at the back
of the embroidery, ensuring that the sticky side of
the Vilene is face down. Affix by ironing together.

3 Make a small turning at each end of the
linen band, wrong sides together, and hem
stitch. Press turnings.

4 Fold the hemmed ends back on to the stiff-
ened linen band with wrong sides together to
make a 2in (5cm) overlap. Oversew the top and
bottom edges so that they form a pocket for the
chequebook card cover to slip into. Press turnings.

ALTERNATIVES

■ Use to decorate bed linen, either worked on
linen band and stitched to the edge of a pillowcase
or sheet, or worked directly on to the bed linen
using waste canvas.

■ This design would look wonderful as a pattern
for a belt, particularly if an antique buckle was
added.

■ Use the border pattern to decorate a spectacles
case.

Elizabethan Bookmark and Chequebook Cover

Key
Work the main body of the design in:
 DMC 823 – Dark navy for the bookmark
 DMC 902 – Dark maroon for the chequebook cover
Work details (shaded yellow) in Gold thread D282

'When This You See' Key Rack

This timely reminder should help to locate those 'oh so elusive' keys!
Fun to make, this simple but effective design is sure to be either a perfect gift,
or a welcome addition to your home.

Design size: 7 x 3¹/₂in (18 x 9cm)
Stitch count: 97 x 49

11 x 7¹/₂in (28 x 19cm) grey 14-count Yorkshire Aida
Stranded cottons (floss) as shown in the key
Purchased wooden frame

Use 2 strands of stranded cotton (floss) over 1 block of fabric.

1 Find the centre of the design and work outwards from this point following the chart

2 Stretch, mount and frame as required (for frame shown, see Suppliers on page 127), ensuring that the frame you choose is sturdy enough to accommodate key hooks. Screw in as many brass hooks as you wish to the bottom piece of the frame.

'When This You See' Key Rack
Key   DMC
924   Antique blue
300   Chocolate brown

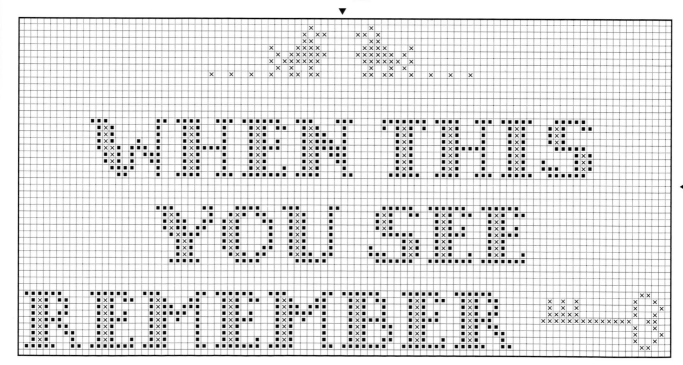

ALTERNATIVES

■ Replace the key motif with the word 'me' for a traditional verse sampler. (You don't even need to chart the word for this, simply use the letters from remember'. Substitute linen for Aida fabric and house in an Oxford frame for an authentic look.

The actual verse on which this design is based is as follows:

> 'When I am dead and in my grave,
> And all my bones are rotten.
> When this you see, remember me,
> Lest I should be forgotten.'

Floral Border Pillowcase

Take a plain white pillowcase and transform it into a thing of beauty with this pretty floral border worked in cross stitch on linen. You could also use 4in (10cm) wide linen band, 28 threads per inch (2.5cm), for this project, though it will make the border design a little bigger.

Strip of white Belfast linen, 32 threads per inch (2.5cm), 4¹/₂in (11.5cm) x the width of your chose pillowcase plus 4in (10cm) for turnings

Stranded cottons (floss) as shown in the key
Tacking (basting) cotton
White 2in (5cm) wide broderie anglaise lace - twice the width of your pillowcase plus 4in (10cm) for turnings
White sewing cotton

Use 2 strands of stranded cotton (floss) over 2 threads of linen.

1 Measure 2in (5cm) from the bottom of the linen strip and begin stitching the border, matching the mid-point on the chart to the mid-point of the strip (widthways).

2 Complete the border in cross stitch, working sufficient length to fit the width of your pillowcase. Trim along the short edge to within ¹/₂in (1cm) of the design.

3 Make ¹/₂in (1cm) turnings with wrong sides together along the long edges of the strip and tack (baste).

4 Pin and tack (baste) the turned edges on to the broderie anglaise lace, covering the raw edge, and at the same time, making small tucks in the lace at short intervals to give a slight fullness.

5 Turn under and tack (baste) the short edges of the linen strip. Neaten the edges of the lace with a narrow hem.

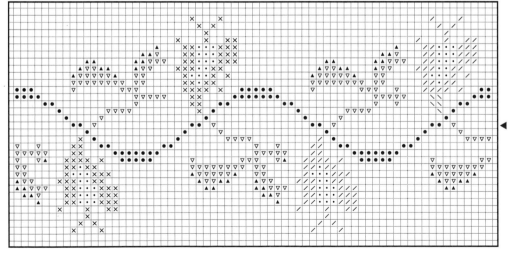

Floral Border

Key	DMC	
••	632	Mid brown
▽▽	733	Light sage
⁄⁄	407	Pink/beige
··	818	Very pale pink
▲▲	730	Dark sage
××	926	Light slate blue

6 Position the linen strip with added lace at the opening edge of your pillowcase and tack (baste) into position, being careful not to tack (baste) through all layers.

7 Machine or hand stitch the strip to the pillowcase at the edge of the linen. Remove tacking (basting) stitches, and press.

ALTERNATIVES

■ Use the same idea – that is the border plus lace, to decorate a plain white sheet.

■ Work the border on a piece of linen band and make into a pot pourri sachet.

■ Work the border to decorate towels with a special Aida insert.

House on the Hill Sampler

This sampler, worked in cross stitch on linen, has a bold alphabet with a myriad of motifs. Stitch and enjoy it in its entirety or pick out several of the motifs to use in different ways. The projects on the following pages will give you some ideas, but, as you can see, the possibilities are endless!

Design size: 18 x 9½in (45.5 x 24cm)
Stitch count: 252 x 132

22 x 14in (56 x 35.5cm) cream evenweave linen, 28
threads per inch (2.5cm)
Stranded cottons (floss) as shown in the key

Use 2 strands of stranded cotton (floss) over 2
threads of linen.

1 Find the centre of the design and work out
wards from this point following the chart.

2 Substitute your own name and the date by
using any of the alphabets on pages 114-115
(Use the numerals from this chart.)

3 Stretch, mount and frame as required (see
pages 118-122).

Birds and Flowers

Charming in its simplicity, this small birds and flowers motif is worked in cross stitch on Rustico fabric. It would make an ideal introduction to cross stitch for a beginner.

Design size: 5¼ x 4½in (13.5 x 11.5cm)
Stitch count: 71 x 62

8¼ x 7½in (21 x 19cm) 14-count Rustico fabric
Stranded cottons (floss) as shown in the key

Use 2 strands of cotton (floss) over 1 block of fabric.

1 Find the centre of the design and work outwards from this point following the chart.

2 Stretch, mount and frame as required (see pages 118-122).

ALTERNATIVES

■ Work the design in wool (yarn) on interlock canvas with 10 holes per inch (2.5cm). Then add a simple border for a stylish sampler cushion.

■ Try working the whole motif in just one space-dyed thread. Add one or two toning motifs and a matching frame.

Key	DMC	
	356	Apricot
	926	Light slate blue
	924	Antique blue
	680	Dark gold
	3371	Very dark brown

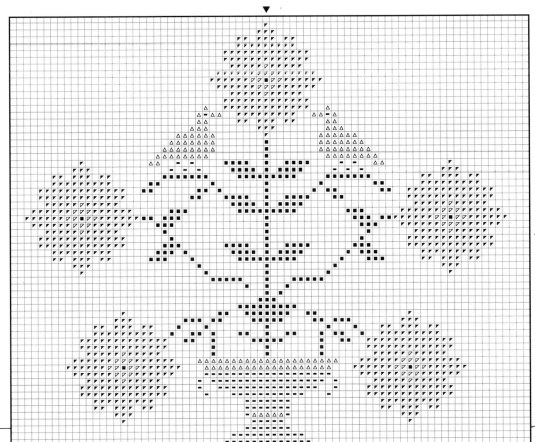

Yellow Birds Sampler

Tiny yellow birds worked in tent stitch on linen and outlined in back stitch adorn this sampler with its traditional border of chrysanthemums.
The main body of the sampler is worked in cross stitch. The initials are an unusual feature, in that they are worked in eyelet stitch with the ground fabric of the sampler (one thread of linen pulled from the edge of the fabric).

Design size: 7³/₄ x 8in (19.5 x 20.5cm)
Stitch count: 99 x 99

12 x 12in (30.5 x 30.5cm) natural Dublin linen, 25 threads per inch (2.5cm)
Stranded cottons (floss) as shown in the key

Use 2 strands of stranded cotton (floss) over 2 threads of linen for the main body of the sampler, and over 1 thread of linen for the yellow birds.

1 Remove two threads from each side edge of the cut linen. These will be used to work your initials in eyelet stitch. Twelve-inch (30.5cm) lengths are perfect for working in this medium as untwisted linen thread is apt to fray if longer lengths are used.

Flora and Fauna Box Lid

By far the most common motifs found on samplers, regardless of age or country, are plants and animals. This design shows a variety of flora and fauna, ranging from stags to birds, and tiny bushes to over-large trees. As is the norm in designs of this kind, scale does not exist! This design is worked entirely in cross stitch on very fine Edinburgh linen.

Design size: 8¹/₂ x 6¹/₂in (21.5 x 16.5cm)
Stitch count: 154 x 112

12¹/₂ x 10¹/₂in (31.5 x 26.5cm) unbleached
Edinburgh linen, 36 threads per inch (2.5cm)
Stranded cottons (floss) as shown in the key
Purpose-made wooden box with a lid to take an
embroidery 9 x 7in (23 x 18cm) (see Suppliers,
page 127)

Use 1 strand of stranded cotton (floss) over 2
threads of linen.

1 Find the centre of the design and work outwards from this point following the chart.

2 Fit the embroidery into the box lid following
the manufacturer's instructions.

ALTERNATIVES

■ This design would translate most successfully to
canvaswork for use either as a cushion, or for a
stool-top.

■ Many of the motifs could be used individually
as designs for greetings cards, pincushions, etc.

■ If one or more alphabets were added at the top
of the design and, perhaps, a border to surround
it, this would make a stunning spot motif sampler,
offering a real challenge to an experienced
embroiderer.

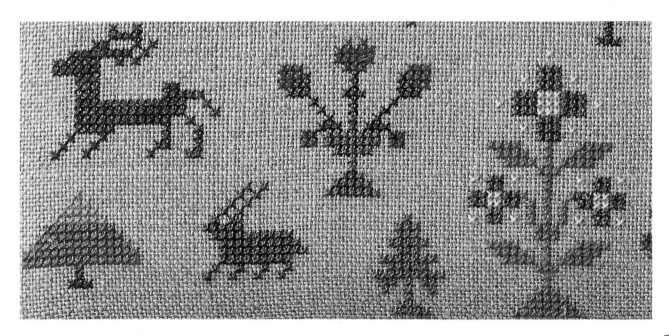

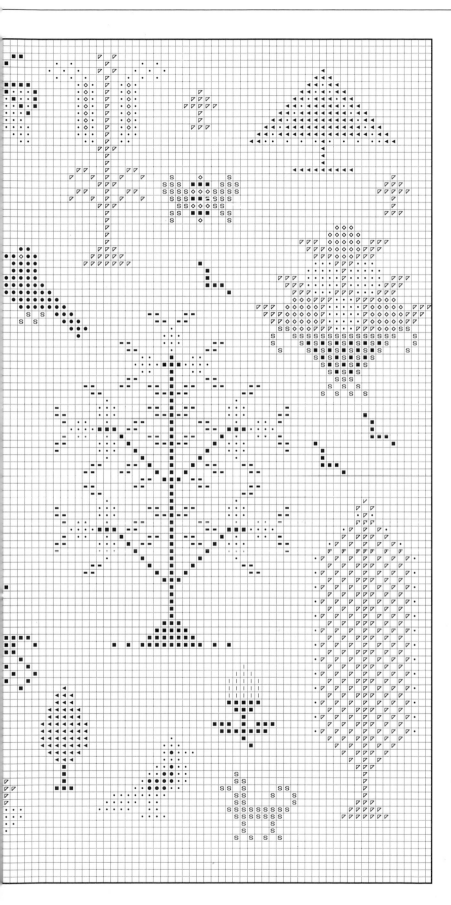

Flora and Fauna Box Lid

Key	DMC	
■■	938	Dark brown
· ·	355	Dark rust
◄◄	732	Sage green
SS	434	Warm brown
• •	413	Dark grey
= =	3051	Dull green
⫼⫼	733	Light sage green
◊ ◊	748	Very pale beige
▽▽	890	Dark green

Birds in a Bower

This pretty birds in a bower motif is extremely versatile and can be used in a number of different ways. Two versions are shown here with a strong contrast in presentation.

'Rustic' Birds in a Bower
Design size: 3⁵⁄₈ x 3¹⁄₄in (9 x 8cm)
Stitch count: 65 x 58

6 x 5¹⁄₂in (15 x 14cm) 18-count Rustico fabric
Stranded cottons (floss) as shown in the key

Use 2 strands of cotton (floss) over 1 block of fabric.

'Silhouette' Birds in a Bower
Design size: 2¹⁄₈ x 1⁷⁄₈in (5.5 x 4.5cm)

5 x 5in (12.5 x 12.5cm) white Belfast linen, 32 threads per inch (2.5cm)
DMC black stranded cotton (floss) 310

Use 1 strand of cotton (floss) over 1 thread of linen.

1 Find the centre of the design and work out-wards from this point following the chart.

2 Stretch, mount and frame as required (see page 118-122).

ALTERNATIVES

■ Use the design for a pincushion – in either wool (yarn) on canvas or stranded cotton (floss) on linen or Aida.

■ Add initials (choose from the alphabets given on pages 114-115) and make up as a greetings card. Use either a purpose-made card, or make your own.

■ Use the design as a centre panel for a cushion. This would look particularly striking if worked in black on white and surrounded with black and white 'log cabin' patchwork.

■ Work in pastel colours for a small wedding sampler. Add the bride's and groom's names or initials on either side of the base, and the date and the name of the church underneath, using a small backstitch alphabet (see pages 114-115).

Birds in a Bower

Key	DMC			
■■	413	Dark grey	◇◇ 926	Light slate blue
▲▲	356	Apricot	×× 407	Pink/beige

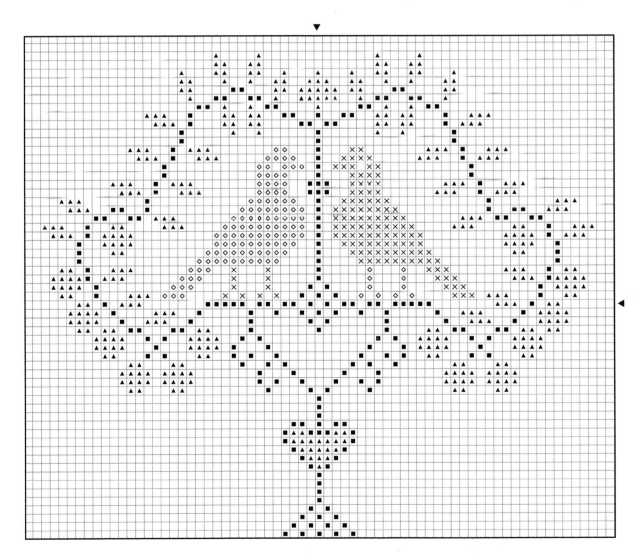

Blackwork Sampler

*Blackwork is sometimes referred to as Spanish work,
in the mistaken belief that it was Catherine of Aragon who introduced
it to this country. In fact, she merely popularised a style of
embroidery which had been worked here since the 15th century.
The stitch used was known as double running stitch but is now referred to
as Holbein stitch, due to the number of times it appears in
the paintings of Holbein, depicting the heavily embroidered dress
of the Tudor period.*

Design size: 5$\frac{1}{4}$ x 13$\frac{1}{4}$in (13.5 x 33.5cm)
Stitch count: 66 x 164

*9 x 17in (23 x 43cm) cream Dublin linen, 25 threads
per inch (2.5cm)*
DMC stranded cotton (floss) Black 310
DMC Gold thread D282

See specific instructions for numbers of threads
to use.

1 Find the centre of the design and work outwards from this point following the chart.

2 Choose your initials and numerals from those
given on pages 114-115. Work out your

details in pencil on graph paper and position as
shown on the chart.

3 Stretch, mount and frame as required (see
pages 118-122).

ALTERNATIVES

■ Choose any of the borders or patterns shown
and incorporate them into your own sampler.
Although it is called 'blackwork', this type of
embroidery was frequently worked in red or blue
and looks just as effective in colour.

■ The pattern just below the initials in the centre
of the design would look stunning if worked as a
border on white linen napkins. You could even
include your initials as shown for added impact.

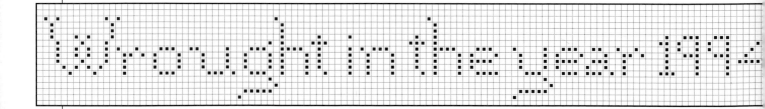

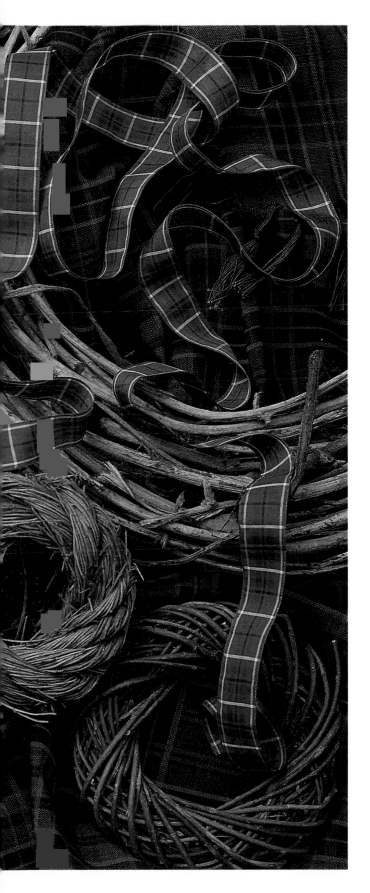

Victorian Alphabet

This simple Victorian alphabet design is worked in cross stitch on linen using space-dyed thread. Although this is a very modern thread, it certainly gives a very Victorian feel to the design.

Design size: 6⅝ x 5½in (17 x 14cm)
Stitch count: 93 x 77

10½ x 9½in (27 x 24cm) cream 28-count Quaker cloth
One skein Wildflowers, colour Ruby from the Caron collection

Use 1 strand of thread over 2 threads of linen.

1   Find the centre of the design and work outwards from this point following the chart.

2   Stretch, mount and frame as required (see pages 118-122).

ALTERNATIVES

■ Use any of the letters of the alphabet to decorate items of clothing, using waste canvas (see page 122).

■ Replace the alphabet with a Victorian verse or motto, for example, 'Improve thy time, Now in thy prime' or 'Patience is a virtue', etc.

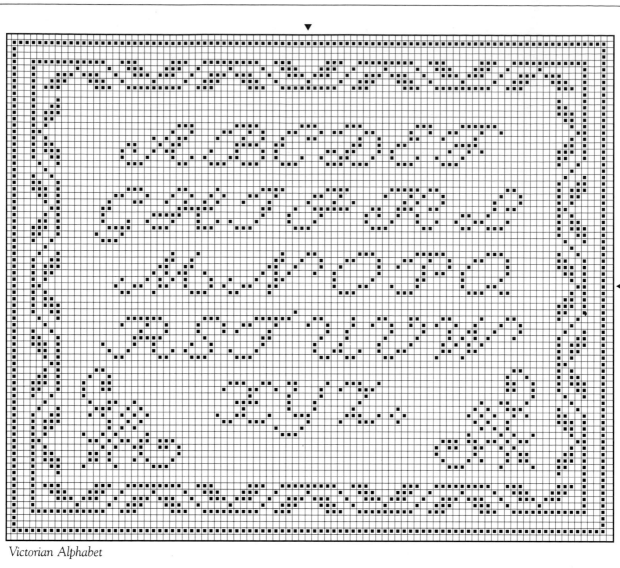

Victorian Alphabet

Initialled Needlecase Lid Alphabet

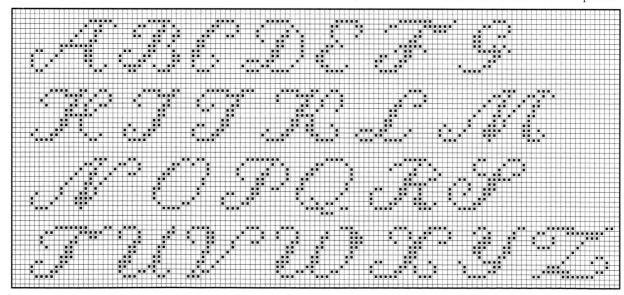

Initialled Needlecase Lid

Very Victorian in flavour, the design adorning the lid of this charming wooden needlecase is worked in tent stitch using variegated silk thread, although you could use stranded cotton (floss) if you prefer.

Design size: 2³/₄ x 1³/₈in (7 x 3.5cm)
Stitch count: 81 x 37

5 x 3in (12.5 x 7.5cm) cream Belfast linen,
32 threads per inch (2.5cm)
Variegated silk thread in blue/grey/brown from
Brethyn Brith, or use DMC variegated stranded cot-
ton (floss) 91 and 105, varying the lengths to achieve
the effect shown
Wooden needlecase (Framecraft)
Glue/impact adhesive

Use 1 strand of variegated silk thread or 2 strands
of stranded cotton (floss) over 1 thread of linen.

1 Find the centre of your chosen initial from the alphabet chart opposite and match to the centre of the main chart. Mark the position lightly on the chart in pencil, then match to the centre of the fabric. Begin work at this point and stitch following the chart.

2 When the embroidery is complete, fit it into the needlecase lid, following the manu- facturer's instructions.

3 Make a twisted cord (see Finishing Techniques, page 121) using four lengths of the variegated silk or two lengths of cotton (floss). Trim to size and glue to the outside edge of the embroidered panel where it meets the wood, start- ing and finishing at the bottom in the middle.

ALTERNATIVES

■ Work the design in cross stitch over two threads of linen (this will double the size), trim the linen to an oval shape, allowing an inch (2.5cm) around the design, and trim with lace to make a pretty dressing table mat.

■ Use the design to decorate an oval trinket pot lid.

■ Use the flower motif singly to add impact to an initial.

■ Using waste canvas (see page 122), use the design to decorate clothing – a pocket on a dress or blouse, or the front of a sweatshirt, for example.

Initialled Needlecase Lid Border

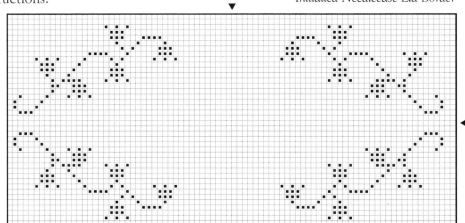

Strawberry Pincushion

A simple repeat motif of a strawberry adorns this easy-to-make pincushion. Worked in tent stitch with crewel wool (yarn) and stranded cotton (floss) on canvas, this decorative pincushion would make a wonderful gift for a friend who enjoys embroidery, or simply to use as a decorative piece in its own right.

Design size: 4³/₄in (12cm) diameter

7 x 7in (18 x 18cm) yellow 22-count petit point canvas
DMC crewel wool (Medici) and stranded cotton (floss) as shown in the key
4¹/₄in (10cm) wooden pincushion base

Use 1 strand of crewel wool (yarn), or 2 strands of stranded cotton (floss) where appropriate, over 1 thread of canvas.

1 Draw a 4¹/₄in (12cm) circle centrally on the canvas in felt-tip pen. As tent stitch tends to distort fabric, the use of a frame is advisable.

2 Stitch the strawberry motif design, working from the chart until the whole area has been covered. Use short lengths of wool (yarn) as it frays very quickly, and this will result in uneven coverage.

3 Remove from the frame and fit the embroidery into the pincushion base, following the manufacturer's instructions.

ALTERNATIVES

■ Work the design as above, but increase the size of the circle and use for a footstool.

■ Work the design in cross stitch on a larger mesh canvas to make a cushion, repeating the motif until the desired size is achieved.

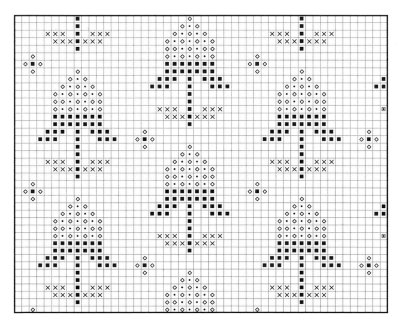

Strawberry Pincushion
Key   DMC Crewel wool (Medici)

◇◇ / ◇◇   8100 Maroon

■■ / ■■   8403 Dark green

×× / ××   8401 Bright sage green

850   Beige (background)

DMC Stranded cotton

⋮⋮   744   Pale yellow

House Picture

Houses such as this are much in evidence on samplers of the 18th and 19th centuries. Often the worker would portray her own house (or school in some cases), thus recording it for posterity. This design, worked in tent stitch on linen, will afford you the same opportunity, either to work the house shown and your own house name, or number and road, etc, or, if you wish, you could chart a design of your own house (see page 122 for help and advice), and substitute this for the one shown.

Design size: 2¹/₂ x 3¹/₂ in (6.5 x 9cm) with house name
Stitch count: 71 x 78 (without house name)

5¹/₂ x 7in (14 x 18cm) cream evenweave linen, 28 threads per inch (2.5cm)
Stranded cottons (floss) as shown in the key

Use 2 strands of stranded cotton (floss) over 1 thread of linen.

1 Find the centre of the design and work outwards from this point following the chart. As tent stitch tends to distort fabric, the use of a frame is advisable.

2 Chart your own house name (or number and road, etc) using the small backstitch alphabet and numerals on page 114-115. Work out your details on graph paper in pencil and position as shown.

3 Stretch, mount and frame as required (see pages 118-122).

ALTERNATIVES

■ In place of the house name, substitute 'Welcome to your new home'. Either frame as a small picture, or use as a design for a greetings card.

■ Double the size of the design by working in cross stitch over two threads of linen. Add not only your house, but also your family details and a simple border. The design is then transformed into a very effective family record sampler.

■ Work the design in cross stitch with wool on a large mesh canvas and make up as a cushion. You could work the design on a rug canvas using several lengths of wool to make a really large floor cushion.

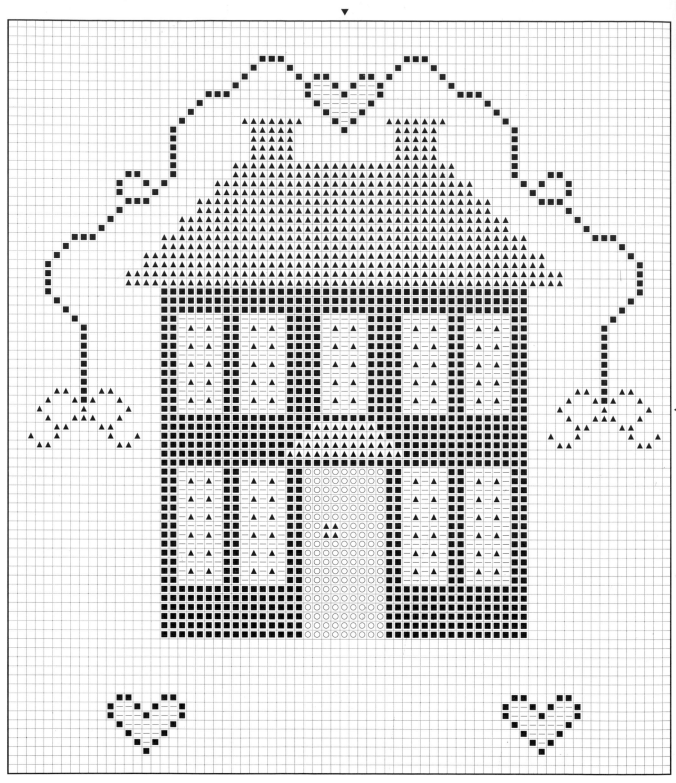

House Picture

Key   DMC

▨▨ 355   Dark rust   ▲▲ 322   Mid blue
▨▨   ▲▲

⊟⊟ 407   Pink/beige   ⊙⊙ 356   Apricot
⊟⊟   ⊙⊙

'Bristol Orphanage' Bookmark and Pincushion

The 'Bristol Orphanage' Samplers, made from about 1820 and consisting mainly of alphabets, numerals, narrow border patterns and corner motifs, were worked in red silk on very closely woven linen.
A great many of these intricate samplers showing strict economy of material still survive, and serve as a gruelling reminder that embroidery was not always a labour of love. Girls as young as five would work one or more of these samplers as preparation for a life in service, part of their duties being the marking of household linen.

The Bookmark
Design size: 1³/₄ x 6¹/₂ in (4.5 x 16.5cm)
Stitch count: 30 x 117

Purchased bookmark
Stranded cotton (floss) as shown in the key

Use 2 strands of stranded cotton (floss) over 1 block of fabric.

THE BOOKMARK

1 Find the mid-point of the bookmark by folding in half and half again. Match to the mid-point of the design and work from this point outwards following the chart.

2 Choose your initials from the alphabets charts on pages 114-115 and position as shown.

The Pincushion
Design size: 3¹/₂ x 3¹/₄ in (9 x 8cm)
Stitch count: 52 x 51

6 x 6in (15 x 15cm) white Belfast linen, 32 threads per inch (2.5cm)
Stranded cotton (floss) as shown in the key
50in (127cm) white cotton lace, 2¹/₂ in (6.5cm) wide
White sewing thread
6 x 6in (15 x 15cm) white cotton backing fabric
Small amount of polyester filling

Use 2 strands of stranded cotton (floss) over 1 block of fabric.

THE PINCUSHION

1 Find the centre of the design and work outwards from this point following the chart.

2 Choose your initials from the alphabets chart on pages 114-115 and position as shown.

3 Machine or hand stitch the two short ends of the lace together and either oversew or zig-zag to neaten. Gather along the straight edge

Overleaf: 'Bristol Orphanage' Bookmark and Pincushion.

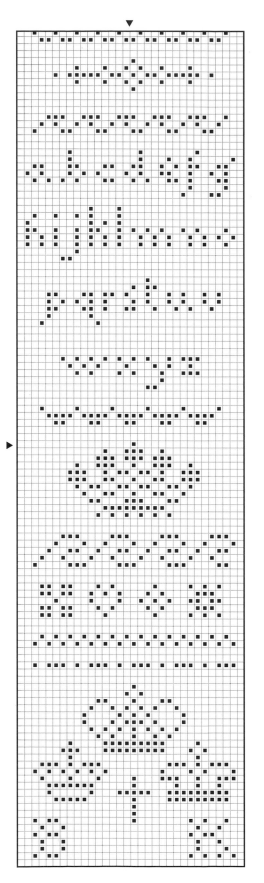

of the lace either by machine or hand, then pin and tack (baste) the gathered edge, with right sides facing, to the embroidered fabric, easing the gathers as you go.

4 Making sure that the frilled edge of the lace is pointing towards the centre of the work (you may like to tack [baste] this edge down so that it does not catch in the seam), place the backing fabric right sides facing on top of the work, matching the edges together. Pin, tack (baste) and then machine through all layers ½in (1.5cm) from the edge, leaving a 2in (5cm) opening for turning. Remove tacking (basting) stitches.

5 Turn and, after filling, close the opening with invisible stitches.

ALTERNATIVES
■ Work the design as shown on the bookmark, mount on velvet-covered card and frame.

■ Work the pincushion design on fine linen and frame in a simple wooden frame for a charming miniature sampler.

■ Incorporate the alphabets, borders and motifs into a larger, more complex design to emulate the Bristol Orphanage Samplers of the past.

Bristol Orphanage Bookmark
Key   DMC
347   Dull red

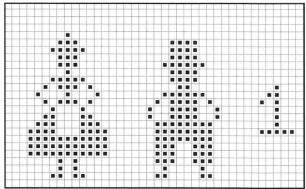

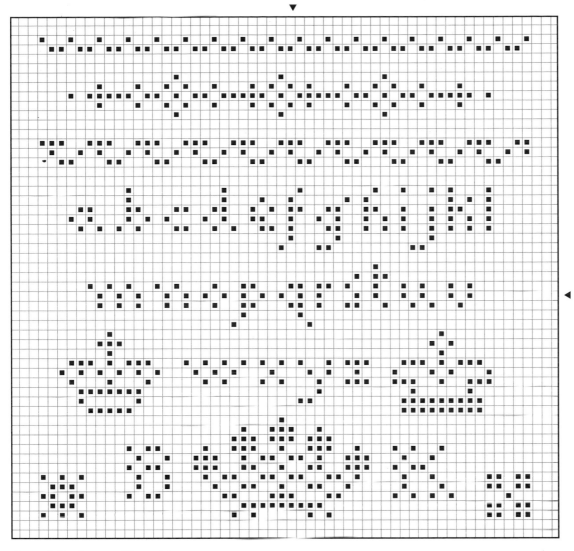

Bristol Orphanage Pincushion
Key DMC
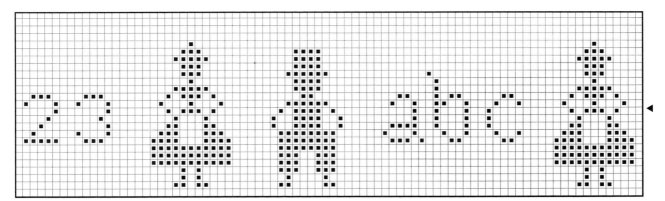 347 Dull red

Sampler Folk *(chart for projects on pages 108-109)*

Sampler Folk

Take the simplest of motifs –
a boy and a girl – add an abc and
a 123 and you have the basis
for any number of charming folk art
designs. No sizes or instructions
are given for these projects, they are
merely meant to inspire you.

By experimenting with a wide
variety of fabrics, threads and ways
of display, you will be able to use
the chart (on pages 106-107) to
create dozens of small projects that
can be completed quickly and
easily. All the projects shown
here are worked in cross stitch,
but you could of course work the
design in a variety of stitches
which will further add to its
versatility.

Sampler Motif Book
Sampler

This sampler - a conglomeration of motifs, borders and alphabets from the book - is really an example of what this book is all about. Why not try putting together your own sampler, a commemorative one for example, in the same way? Or, if you do not feel competent enough at this stage to tackle a complete design, try swapping and changing some motifs around and your finished sampler will be a piece that is unique to you. Confidence will be gained with practice, and by using the book in this way, you will be able to create unlimited designs of your own.

Design size: 8 1/4 x 10 3/4 in (21 x 27.5cm)
Stitch count: 107 x 137

14 1/2 x 16 3/4 in (36 x 42.5cm) 25 count unbleached Dublin linen
Stranded cotton (floss) as shown in the key

Work in cross stitch using two strands of cotton (floss) over two threads of linen.

1 Find the centre of the design and work outwards from this point following the chart.

2 Stretch, mount and frame as required (see pages 118-122)

ALTERNATIVES

■ Use any combination of motifs from this book to create a unique design.

■ Substitute the alphabet with names or a motto to personalise your sampler.

DMC

		730	Sage green			738	Beige
		500	Dark green			407	Beige/pink
		434	Warm brown			926	Slate blue
		315	Plum			3371	Very dark brown
		918	Rust			924	Antique blue

Symbolism of Sampler Motifs

Adam and Eve: *Good and evil*

Angels: *Martyrdom*

Apple: *Love/fertility*

Bee: *Chastity/Virgin Mary*

Butterfly or moth: *Immortality/Resurrection*

Candle or candlestick: *Devotion/prayer*

Carnation (pink): *Maternal love*

Cat: *Idleness*

Cherry: *Fruit of heaven*

Cock: *Watchfulness/penitence*

Columbine: *The Holy Spirit*

Cross: *Faith*

Crown: *Hope/eternity*

Crowned cross: *Eternity*

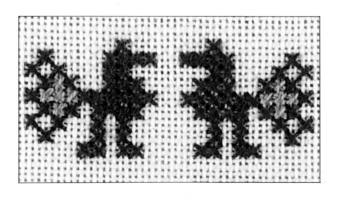

Daffodil or leek: *Wales*

Dog: *Fidelity*

Dove: *Mercy/peace*

Duck: *Marital fidelity*

Eagle: *Empire or the Ascension (in Christian symbolism)*

Falcon: *Pride/nobility*
Garland: *Victory/merit*
Goose: *Stupidity/gullibility*
Hare: *Timidity*
Harp or lyre: *Purity/music*
Hart: *Baptism/gentleness and pride*
Heart: *Charity*
Honeysuckle: *Enduring faith*
Horse: *Fertility*
Lily: *Purity*
Lion: *Strength*
Marigold: *Obedience*
Monkey: *Laziness/mischief*
Olive: *Peace/goodwill*
Owl: *Wisdom*
Parrot: *Gossip*
Peacock: *Vanity*
Pelican: *Resurrection*
Pomegranate: *Hope/eternal life*
Rabbit: *Gentleness*

Rose: *Love/patience/beauty*
Shamrock: *Ireland*
Ship: *Journey*
Snake: *Reward/wickedness*
Squirrel: *Mischief*
Stork: *Parental love/bringer of happiness*
Strawberry: *Perfect righteousness*
Swan: *Love*
Thistle: *Scotland*
Tortoise: *Strength/slowness*

Tree of Life: *Immortality*
Tulip: *Perfect love*
Unicorn: *Chastity/purity*
Violet and daisy: *Humility/modesty*
Weathercock: *Preacher*
Weeping willow: *Sorrow/unhappiness*

Finishing Techniques

Before taking your embroidery to the framers or framing it yourself, it is advisable to run through the following check list

1 Always make a point of checking the completed design against the chart as it is so easy to miss out stitches, or even whole areas of a design!

2 Turn your work over and check for loose, trailing threads. Check that the threads are secure, then snip off as close to the work as possible. Dark-coloured trailing threads in particular will show through light fabric and spoil the appearance of the finished work.

3 Unless your work has become really grubby in the working, avoid washing and ironing. Embroidery always looks better without this process. If you have taken the necessary steps to protect it while in progress, and have used an embroidery frame or hoop (one that is large enough to encompass not only the work but also to allow a reasonable margin for framing), and taken the trouble to store it in a clean white pillowcase, for example, when not in use, then washing should not be necessary. If, however, it is necessary, wash by hand with mild soap flakes, taking great care not to rub or wring. Simply swish the embroidery about in the water. Rinse well, then roll in a clean white towel. Open out and leave to dry. To press, lay several layers of towelling on an ironing board. Lay the work face down on the towels, cover with a clean white cloth and press with a warm iron. This method prevents the stitches from becoming flattened. Do not iron plastic canvas or perforated paper.

Stretching and Mounting Your Work

This part of the finishing process is vital as the most wonderful piece of work can be totally ruined if it is puckered or creased. It is always worth going to the trouble of finishing your work properly by stretching and mounting (unless it is very tiny indeed).

1 Use a strong, acid-free mount board (available from good art shops) or hardboard (covered with acid-free paper). Measure your work and cut the board slightly bigger than your embroidery if a mount is to be used or, if not, to the size of your chosen frame.

2 Place the card or covered hardboard on the wrong side of the embroidery and, when in

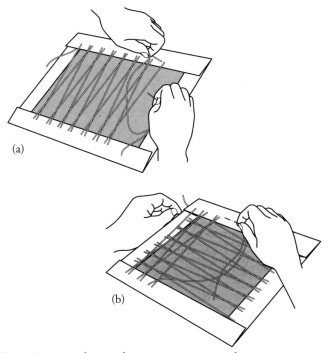

Fig 1: Lacing technique for mounting your work.

position, secure with straight pins inserted into the edge. Turn frequently to check that the embroidery remains correctly placed.

3 Fold over the side edges of the fabric, then use a long length of strong thread (fine crochet cotton is ideal) to lace back and forth (Fig 1a). Pull up the stitches to tighten and secure firmly.

4 Complete the top and bottom in the same way (Fig 1b).

Blocking (or Stretching) Canvaswork

If you have not used a frame (or sometimes even if you have), canvaswork can become badly distorted and will need stretching back into shape. You will need: a piece of thick wooden board, larger than your embroidery and soft enough to take drawing pins or tacks), several sheets of newspaper or blotting paper, plain white porous paper on which you have drawn the outline size of your embroidery in waterproof pen, and brass drawing pins or tacks.

Lay the sheets of paper on the wooden board and wet them thoroughly, a plant spray is ideal for this purpose. On top of this, lay the sheet of white paper with the size of your design marked on it. Lay the embroidery right side up centrally on top of this and, starting at top centre, insert the drawing pins at intervals of approximately 1in (25mm), working outwards and stretching the canvas as you go. Pin along the bottom edge in the same way and then the sides. Leave the canvas to dry thoroughly – this could take as long as two or three days. If the canvas was badly distorted, it may be necessary to repeat the whole process.

Decorative Mounts

Although, traditionally, samplers were framed without a card mount surrounding the design (the reason for this being that they were primarily a functional piece of work), there is really no reason

why modern samplers have to follow the same pattern. Obviously, if you choose to work a very traditional design and you want it to look authentic, then the addition of a card mount would be inappropriate, but since the reason for working a sampler today has changed to one of relaxation and enjoyment and the use of the finished piece to one of decoration, there is no reason not to enhance the design in any way you choose.

Fabric-covered Mounts

The technique of covering a mount with fabric means that you need not restrict yourself to a plain uninteresting mount that does not always do justice to your work. Virtually any colour, pattern or texture is possible with this method. You will need: strong card, fabric, glue/impact adhesive, a metal ruler, a scalpel or craft knife, and a cutting board or several layers of card to protect the surface you are cutting on. If you are making a padded mount, you will also need one or two layers of terylene wadding (batting).

Covering a Mount with Fabric

1 Measure the completed embroidery carefully and cut the mount and the aperture to the size required. Round, oval and, in particular, heart-shaped apertures are very difficult to cut perfectly and, even though you are covering with fabric, uneven edges will show. Unless you are very skilled it is best to ask your picture framer to cut these for you.

2 Cut the fabric to the size of the mount plus allowances for turnings. The allowances will vary according to the size of the mount and also the type of the fabric chosen (for example, because of its thickness, velvet will require a larger allowance than fine cotton). Always make sure that you align the mount with the straight grain of the fabric.

3 Place the fabric right side down and position the mount in the middle. If making a padded mount, cut the padding to the same size as the

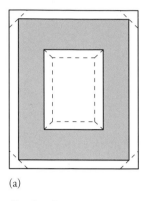
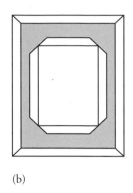

(a)   (b)

Fig 2a: Covering a mount with fabric.

mount and place between the fabric and the card. Snip off the corners of the fabric as shown by the dotted lines in Fig 2a.

4 Apply adhesive to the remaining fabric at the outer edge. Fold over and press flat.

5 To cut out the inside 'window', first cut out the rectangle as shown by the dotted lines and then carefully snip into the corners, stopping just short of the edge. Apply adhesive to this remaining fabric, fold over and press flat.

6 Apply any further embellishments you may like to add – bows, sequins, braids, etc – and then carefully align the mount over the embroidery. Fix with glue or masking tape.

Framing

The correct choice of frame can, quite simply, make or break a piece of work. A relatively simple piece can be greatly enhanced or even transformed with a carefully chosen frame and/or mount. It is important, therefore, not to rush this process, but to take some time to consider all the possibilities. You may have spent many hours on the work to be framed, so it would be sacrilege at this stage to spoil it with an inappropriate frame. You need not go to great expense, however; often a coat of paint is all that is needed to transform a relatively dull frame. Choose colours which compliment the worked piece. 'Match-Pots', those small pots of paint available from DIY shops for trying out colours, are an excellent choice, as they

are relatively inexpensive and will enable you to experiment by mixing colours to achieve the desired shade if necessary. For a stippled effect, simply paint the frame in one colour, then dip an old toothbrush in a contrasting colour and run your finger along the bristles to flick the paint on to the frame (be sure to protect the surrounding area with plenty of newspaper!). There are also many coloured varnishes available that will greatly enhance a plain frame. Try matching one of them to the main colour of your design.

Unless your work has a very raised surface or is very textured, the use of glass is advisable as this will protect the work from dust, dirt and inquisitive fingers! Your framer will probably ask you to choose between plain or non-reflective glass. Non-reflective glass certainly sounds the obvious choice, but has a rather mottled and flat appearance which tends to dull colours. Plain glass will show your work to much better advantage. If you have decided to use glass but are not using a mount, ask your picture framer to use thin strips of card to prevent the glass coming into contact with your needlework. This will stop it from flattening your stitches.

Making a Fold-over Card

A great variety of ready-made fold-over cards are now available from art and needlework shops (see suppliers on page 127). If, however, the size or colour you want is not available, the following instructions will enable you to make your own.

1 Choose thin card in a colour to match your design.

2 Measure your embroidery to assess the size and shape of the aperture. (Round, oval and heart-shaped apertures are much more difficult to cut accurately unless you have great skill.) Do not attempt to cut any aperture with scissors, always use a craft knife or scalpel.

3 Cut your card to the size and shape required (Fig 3a). Cut an aperture in the middle section 'B' and, using a craft knife, lightly score fold lines as indicated by the dotted lines.

(a)

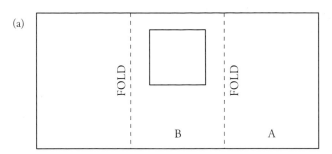

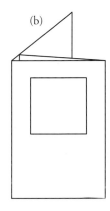

Fig 3: How to make a fold over card.

4 Position the aperture over your embroidery. Trim away any excess fabric and glue into position or secure with double-sided sticky tape.

5 Fold 'A' over 'B' and glue together (Fig 3b).

How to Make a Tassel

1 Cut a piece of stiff card to the length you wish the tassel to be. Wind the thread around the card until the required thickness is achieved. If you are making a set of tassels, keep count of the number of times you wind around the card, so that all the tassels will be the same.

2 Thread a needle with a long piece of the same colour thread. Pass it under the wound threads at the top, next to the card, and tie securely leaving two trailing threads of the same length. Do not fasten off.

3 Cut the bound threads at the bottom of the card to release them.

4 Thread both of the ends used to tie the tassel into the needle, pass through the top of the tassel and bring out about ¹/₂ in (1.5cm) down (less for a smaller tassel).

5 Wind the thread tightly several times around the tassel to form the head. Knot securely and pass the needle back through the bound threads to the top. Use this remaining thread to attach the tassel to the article.

How to Make a Twisted Cord

1 Assess the length of cord required and cut a length of thread three times as long.

2 Make a loop in each end of the thread and attach one end to a hook or doorknob.

3 Slip a pencil through the other end and, keeping the thread taut, begin twisting the pencil round and round until, when released, the thread begins to twist back on itself.

4 Keeping the threads taut, fold the length in half, matching the ends together. Stroke along the cord to even out the twists. Finally, tie the ends together. If a thicker cord is required, simply use more strands.

Charting Names and Dates

If you wish to personalise your work, for example by adding a name and date, this is relatively easy to do. Work out your details in pencil on graph paper, adjusting the space to suit the letter chosen. For example, a lower case i placed next to a lower case l usually looks better with two spaces between if the alphabet is very plain (even if only one space is allowed between the other letters). This type of adjustment will sometimes be necessary between other letters but this will quickly become apparent during the charting process. When you have worked out your details, count the number of squares used vertically and horizontally and position the lettering evenly and centrally in the appropriate place on your fabric. You could also mark the position of your details lightly in pencil on the chart itself to ensure that they are correctly positioned.

Charting Your Own Designs

If you want to substitute a design (for example your own house for the one shown in the House Picture, page 102), you can easily achieve this.

1 Take a good colour photograph of your home face on.

2 If necessary, enlarge the design on a photocopier to the size you wish the finished work to be. There are now many shops that offer this facility.

3 Place a sheet of tracing graph paper over the design. This is available in various counts which correspond to the thread count of fabric, so if, for example, you wish to work on 14-count Aida,

choose 14-count tracing graph paper. Trace the design on to the graph paper, squaring up the design and eliminating any unnecessary details.

4 Colour in the design using coloured crayons. The chart is now ready to stitch from.

Using Waste Canvas

Waste canvas can be successfully used to apply a charted design to fabric without an evenweave. Simply cut a piece of waste canvas slightly bigger than the overall finished design size and tack (baste) into position onto the right side of the chosen fabric or item of clothing.

Find the centre of your charted design and match this to the centre of the piece of canvas and fabric. When completed, spray the whole design with water and using tweezers, remove the soaked threads of the canvas one by one. Leave the finished embroidery to dry and press on the wrong side.

Stitch Directory

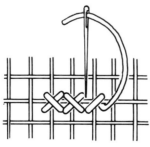

Cross stitch over one thread

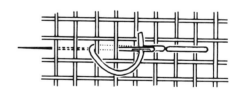

Back stitch

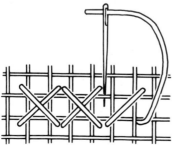

Cross stitch over two threads

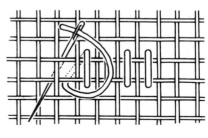

Satin stitch

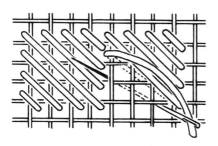

Reversed cushion stitch

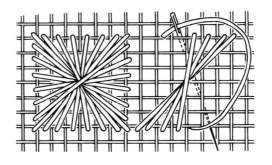

Rhodes stitch

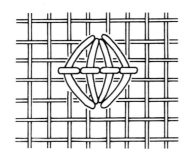

Queen stitch

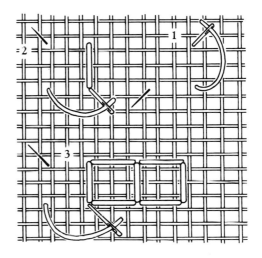

Four-sided stitch

 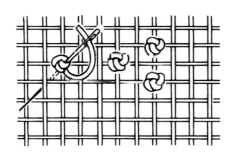

French knot

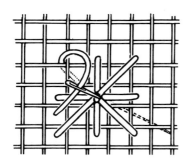

Eyelet stitch/Algerian eye

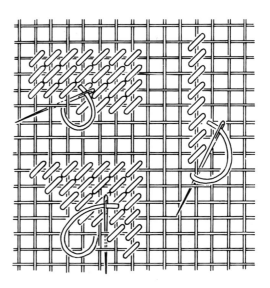

Tent stitch

Conversion Chart

DMC	Anchor	DMC	Anchor	DMC	Anchor	DMC	Anchor	DMC	Anchor	DMC	Anchor	DMC	Anchor
Blanc	1	415	398	611	898	778	968*	898	359	972	298	3685	69
Ecru	387	420	374	612	832	780	310	899	(40)	973	290	3687	68
208	111	422	943	613	853	781	309*	900	(326)*	975	370	3688	66
209	109	433	371	632	936	782	308	902	72	976	(309)*	3689	49
210	108	434	365	640	393*	783	307	904	258	977	313	3705	35
211	342	435	901*	642	392	791	178	905	257	986	246	3706	33
221	897	436	363	644	396	792	177	906	256	987	244	3708	31
223	895*	437	362	645	273*	793	176	907	255	988	243	3712	10*
224	893	444	291	646	8581*	794	175	910	230*	989	242	3713	968*
225	892	445	288	647	8581*	796	133	911	230*	991	(189)	3716	25
300	352	451	233	648	900*	797	132	912	205	992	187*	3721	896*
301	349*	452	232	666	46	798	131	913	204	993	186*	3722	895*
304	47	453	231	676	891	799	145	915	972	995	410	3726	970
307	289	469	267*	677	300*	800	144	917	89	996	433	3727	969*
309	42	470	266*	680	901*	801	358	918	341*	3011	845	3731	(38)
310	403	471	265	699	229	806	169*	919	340	3012	843	3733	75*
311	148	472	(278)	700	228	807	168*	920	339	3013	842	3740	872
312	979	498	(43)	701	227	809	130	921	338	3021	905*	3743	869
315	(896)*	500	879	702	226	813	160	922	337	3022	(899)*	3746	118*
316	969*	501	878	703	239	814	45	924	851	3023	(899)*	3747	120
317	400	502	877	704	283	815	22	926	850	3024	900*	3750	(123)
318	399	503	876	712	926	816	(44)	927	848	3031	360*	3752	976
320	215	504	875	718	88	817	19	928	847	3032	903*	3753	975
321	9046	517	170	720	326*	818	48	930	922	3033	830	3755	140
322	978	518	(168)*	721	324*	819	271	931	921	3041	871	3756	158*
326	59	519	(167)*	722	323	820	134	932	343	3042	870	3760	161*
327	100	520	862*	725	306	822	390	934	862*	3045	888	3761	9159*
333	119	522	860	726	295	823	150	935	269*	3046	887	3765	169*
334	977	523	859*	727	293	824	164	936	846	3051	861	3766	167*
335	(41)	524	858*	730	924*	825	162	937	268*	3052	859*	3768	779
336	149	535	(273)*	731	281*	826	161*	938	381	3053	858*	3770	276
340	118*	543	933	732	281*	827	9159*	939	152	3064	883	3772	914*
341	117	550	101	733	280*	828	158*	943	188	3072	274	3773	882
347	13*	552	99	734	279	829	906	945	881	3078	292	3774	778*
349	13*	554	97	738	361	830	277*	946	332	3325	129	3776	349*
350	(11)	561	212	739	366	831	277*	947	330	3326	36	3777	20
351	10*	562	210	740	316*	832	907*	948	778*	3328	10*	3778	9575
352	9*	563	208	741	314	833	(907)*	950	4146*	3340	329	3779	868*
353	6	564	206*	742	303	834	874	951	880	3341	328	3781	905*
355	341*	580	924*	743	305	838	380	954	203	3345	268*	3782	831
356	5975	581	28*	744	301	839	360*	955	206*	3346	267*	3787	(393)*
367	(216)	597	168*	745	300*	840	379	956	54	3347	266*	3790	903*
368	214	598	167*	746	386	841	378	957	52	3348	264	3799	236
369	(213)	600	78	747	928	842	376	958	187*	3350	65		
370	856	601	77	754	4146*	844	273*	959	186*	3354	74		
317	855	602	63	758	868*	869	944	961	76	3362	263		
372	854	603	62	760	9*	890	(683)	962	75*	3363	262		
400	351	604	55	761	23	891	29	963	73	3364	260		
402	347	605	50	762	234	892	28	964	185	3371	382		
407	914*	606	335	772	259	893	27	966	240	3607	87		
413	401	608	333	775	128	894	26	970	324*	3608	86		
414	235	610	889	776	24	895	269*	971	316*	3609	85		

italic * indicates that this Anchor shade has been used more than once

Bibliography

Cirker, Blanche (Ed), *Needlework Alphabets and Designs*, Dover (1975)

Clabburn, Pamela, *The Needleworker's Dictionary*, Macmillan (1976)

Colby, Averil, *Samplers*, Batsford (1964)

Crawford, Heather M., *Needlework Samplers of Northern Ireland*, Allingham Publishing (1989)

Deforges, Regine and Dormann, Genevieve, *Alphabets*, Albin Mitchel (1987)

Don, Sarah, *Traditional Samplers*, David & Charles (1986)

Edmonds, Mary Jaene, *Samplers and Samplermakers (An American Schoolgirl Art 1700-1850)*, Rizzoli International Publications, Inc (1991)

Eirwen Jones, Mary, *British Samplers*, Batsford (1948)

The Embroiderers' Guild Practical Library, *Making Samplers*, David & Charles (1993)

Fawdry, Marguerite and Brown, Deborah, *The Book of Samplers*, Lutterworth Press (1980)

Forstner, Regina, *Traditional Samplers*, Rosenheimer Verlaghaus Alfred Forg GmbH & Co (1983)

Hersh, Tandy and Charles, *Samplers of the Pennsylvania Germans*, The Pennsylvania German Society (1991)

Huish, Marcus, *Samplers and Tapestry Embroideries*, Dover (1970)

Kay, Dorothea, *Sew a Sampler*, A&C Black Ltd (1979)

Lammer, Jutta, *Making Samplers (New & Traditional Designs)*, Sterling Publishing Co Inc (1984)

Lewis, Felicity, *Needlepoint Samplers*, Studio Vista (1981)

Meulenbelt-Nieuwburg, Albarta, *Embroidery Motifs from Dutch Samplers*, Batsford (1974)

Pesel, Louisa F., *Historical Designs for Embroidery*, Dover (1970)

Ring, Betty, *American Needlework Treasures*, E.P. Dutton (1987)

Ring, Betty, 'American Samplers and Pictorial Needlework, 1650-1850' *Girlhood Embroidery (vols I & II)*, Alfred A. Knopf, Inc (1993)

Ryan, Patricia and Bragdon, Allen D., *Historic Samplers*, Bulfinch Press (1992)

Sebba, Anne, *Samplers: Five Centuries of a Gentle Craft*, Thames & Hudson (1979)

Snook, Barbara, *English Embroidery*, Mills & Boon Ltd, London (1960)

Stanwood Bolton, Ethel and Johnson Coe, Eva, *American Samplers*, Dover (1973)

Stevens, Christine, *Samplers (From the Welsh Folk Museum Collection)*, Gomer Press (1991)

Swain, Margaret, *Scottish Embroidery*, Batsford (1986)

Acknowledgements

My grateful thanks to the following people for all their help and support:
First and foremost, my wonderfully supportive husband Chris, for always being such a
calming influence (sometimes so calm he seems almost unconscious compared to my harassed self!).
My children Katie and Nicholas – Katie for her wealth of good ideas for 'alternatives', and
Nicholas for preparing the computer charts (when he would much rather be
playing rugby or supporting British Telecom with his excessive custom!).
My wonderful mother-in-law, Irene, and father-in-law, Jim, without whose constant help
and support everything would most certainly grind to a halt!
My agent Doreen Montgomery for all her ongoing help and encouragement.
Everyone at David & Charles for putting everything together so well, and Di Lewis for her
wonderful photography. DMC Creative World for fabric, threads and the linen band for
the guitar strap. Mike Grey at Framecraft Miniatures for trinket pots, bookmarks,
jar lacys and the wooden needlecase. Jane Greenoff for linen band and perforated paper.

Suppliers

Brethyn Brith, Unit 2, Museum of the Welsh Woollen Industry, Drefach-Felindre, Llandysul, Dyfed SA44 5UP – Space-dyed thread

Canopia, PO Box 420, Uxbridge, Middlesex UB8 2GW – Wooden boxes for needlework

Craft Creations Ltd, 1-7 Harpers Yard, Ruskin Road, Tottenham, London N17 8NE – Greetings cards with pre-cut mounts

DMC Creative World, Pullman Road, Wigston, Leicester LE18 2DY – Zweigart fabrics and DMC threads

Falcon Art Supplies, Unit 7, Sedgley Park Trading Estate, George Street, Prestwich, Manchester M25 8WD – Framing

Framecraft Miniatures Ltd, 372-376 Summer Lane, Hockley, Birmingham B19 3QA – Trinket pots, bookmarks, jar lacys, wooden needlecases

Jane Greenoff's Inglestone Collection, Yells Yard, Cirencester Road, Fairford, Gloucestershire G17 4BS – Linen band and perforated paper (stitching paper)

S&A Frames, 12 Humber Street, Cleethorpes, Humberside DN35 8NN – Key rack frame, Oxford frame (House on the Hill Sampler)

Silken Strands, 33 Linksway, Gatley, Cheadle, Cheshire SK8 4LA – Specialist shiny silk and metallic threads

Woodhouse, Rock Channel, Rye, East Sussex TN31 7HJ – Wooden sewing boxes, footstools and tapestry frames

General Needlecraft Suppliers

Campden Needlecraft, High Street, Chipping Campden, Gloucestershire GL55 6AG

Hepatica, 82a Water Lane, Wilmslow, Cheshire SK9 5BB

The Strawberry Sampler, 56 School Lane, Didsbury, Manchester M20 6RT

Voirrey Embroidery, Brimstage Hall, Brimstage, Wirral, Cheshire L63 6JA

When writing to any of the above suppliers, please include a stamped addressed envelope for your reply.

Country Yarns the Sampler Company

Brenda Keyes's sampler charts, complete kits, linen, needlework accessories and 'Country Yarns Thread Organisers' are available from: Country Yarns the Sampler Company, Holly Tree House, Lichfield Drive, Prestwich, Manchester M25 0HX. Please write for details or telephone/fax 0161-773 9330.

Index